THE GIN BOOK

Also by John Doxat

The Complete Drinker's Companion
Practical Cocktails
The Indispensable Drinks Book
Stirred – Not Shaken
The Book of Drinking
Drinks and Drinking
Handbook of Cocktails & Mixed Drinks

* * *

The Living Thames
Israel
Shinwell Talking

JOHN DOXAT, after many years as journalist and editor – and devotee of Gin – had the good fortune to join a major London Gin company, where he was employed for nearly two decades. This happily enabled him to combine regular imbibing with research.

John Doxat is author of eight varied drink books (apart from more general ones) and has contributed many features to newspapers and magazines. A writer in American *Gourmet* once described him as "Britain's foremost thinking drinker". He is particularly pleased to see *The Gin Book* published in the year that marks the 300th anniversary of the introduction of the Act of Parliament that proved to be the foundation of the great British Gindustry.

THE GIN BOOK

John Doxat

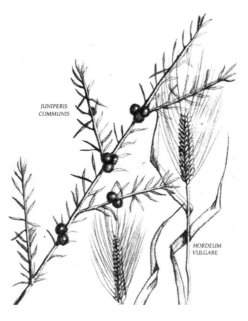

JUNIPERIS COMMUNIS

HORDEUM VULGARE

Quiller Press

This book is respectfully dedicated to
Dame June Ippa,
Patron of the National Institute of Ginocologists,
to whom the author is internally grateful

"Gin and water is the source of all my inspiration."

Lord Byron

First published 1989 by
Quiller Press Ltd
46 Lillie Road, London SW6 1TN

ISBN cased: 0 907621 73 2
paperback: 1 870948 31 9

Design and production in association with
Book Production Consultants, Cambridge

Printed and bound in Yugoslavia by Mladinska Knjiga

C ONTENTS

FOREWORD

Hugely popular, stylish, classy, for those with taste. That's gin. How fortunate that the English acquired the taste for a drink originally produced in Holland in the mid-16th century.

London rapidly increased its reputation for gin distilling and subsequently developed as the international centre for a particularly high quality gin – London Dry.

All is revealed in the following pages of *The Gin Book*, a perceptive insight into the white spirit drink which has found favour and earned respect throughout the world.

John Doxat has done justice to the historically fascinating, yet surprisingly under-reported, role that gin has played in the rich history and development of spirits.

His immense knowledge on the subject, combined with humour and colourful writing style, make for an interesting approach to the second most popular spirit in the world.

Of course, as with sport, art, literature or music, the spirits industry has its important figures; men and women whose determination to pursue the highest standards of craftsmanship give them a special place in the overall story.

As you will read, one such person was Alexander Gordon, the entrepreneur responsible for the world's number one gin, of which four bottles are consumed every second of the day and night.

He noted that many other distilleries were producing inferior gin from poor basic spirits and dubious flavourings, and set out to change all that, using only the finest ingredients blended to a quality formula. And what a resounding success his ideas became. His product met with approval and by 1769 he formed a company.

Alexander Gordon's insistence on quality swiftly gained him a reputation for excellence. His unique recipe remains a secret to this day.

The Gordon's name spread throughout the world via the 'sales executives' of the Merchant and British Navies and a booming export trade ensued. One of the first export orders was from a group of settlers in Australia who arranged for the skippers of ships returning to London to take a consignment of gold dust back with them as payment in advance for a shipment of Gordon's Gin.

The acknowledged versatility of gin has led to its widespread use as the major component of mixed drinks and cocktails. And although gin has a fashionable image, its appeal is widespread.

Gin and tonic has become the classic combination but a wide variety of mixers such as orange, lime, bitter lemon and pineapple, and an even wider range of cocktails is used with, or have as their base, London Dry Gin, epitomised by Gordon's. Gordon's, the best selling brand of its kind, enjoys a huge market to some 150 countries throughout the world.

Another distiller who became known for his excellence was Charles Tanqueray who at the age of 20 established a distillery not far from that of Alexander Gordon at the site of a pure water spring. As with Gordon's, Tanqueray was taken around the British Empire by Colonists and soon gained favour.

Tanqueray has always been at the top end of the prestige category with the distinctive, elegant taste matched by the distinctive bottle based on the shape of a Victorian fire hydrant found on the pavements of old London.

Fashionable in Hollywood with stars such as Frank Sinatra and Bob Hope, Tanqueray has become THE gin for the Dry Martini in the USA; over one million cases are sold there each year and it is the country's number one imported gin. Today, the distinctive green bottle with the red seal is a feature of top bars, hotels and restaurants throughout the world.

Pioneers such as Alexander Gordon and Charles Tanqueray decided that there should be a high grade gin, carefully made from the very best ingredients, available to the people who wanted top quality and who were prepared to pay for that quality.

As distillers, they took enormous pride in perfecting methods of production which thankfully live on to this day. Acknowledged experts such as John Doxat are fully aware of, and appreciate the contribution made by such giants of the spirits industry.

Their efforts and determination, along with others to whom nothing less than perfection was acceptable, will always occupy an important part in the development of a fascinating industry. *The Gin Book* is a testimony to such figures and is an ideal way to enhance your appreciation of one of the most popular drinks in the world.

We are confident that they would have approved wholeheartedly of *The Gin Book*. Happily, John Doxat has captured, with humour and a strong eye for technical and human interest, all the things that have made and make gin an integral part of one of the United Kingdom's most significant industries. This book provides a rare opportunity to acquaint yourself with the background to a versatile drink which went on to become one of the world's favourites.

P. J. Tanqueray
Director
Tanqueray Gordon & Co. Ltd.

*A*PERITIF

It seems odd that, amongst the world's handful of great and enduring spirituous products, gin has received comparatively scant literary attention. Yet, in Britain, gin is second only to Scotch whisky in popularity, and it is well up in the top league of international spirits. Also, gin has a long and fascinating story of development to present status – a Cinderella tale of rags to riches, pleb to peer, pub to palace, which is the best-loved of romances.

To my knowledge, there has only been one full-length publication devoted to gin; very different from this one. So I am filling a bibliographic lacuna, a satisfying task for any author. To this is added my delight in being commissioned to write not a feature, not a chapter, but an entire volume on a product which has been for many happy years my favourite drink – and I could call a hundred witnesses to prove that!

* * *

There were people who told me that "there's not a book in gin: not enough to say". I was sure they were wrong, even when it was gin-drinkers who were saying it. I had already written a great deal about gin, but I had never been able to give it the length of treatment it merits. Others tried to discourage me: "There arn't enough people interested in gin to justify a book." I have never believed that. World gin sales are enormous. I do not know how many gin-drinkers, regular or occasional, there are in my own country – three million? five million? Or in the U.S.A. – ten million? twenty million? And in English-speaking countries – umpteen million; to say nothing of other lands. Assuming that it is only a small proportion of these throngs who are perceptive drinkers, interested in knowledge, and that only a minor percentage of those find this book, the potential readership is nonetheless numerically formidable.

Satisfied on the viability of my project from an authorship viewpoint, like an Everest climber or round-the-world yachtsman, I looked for a sponsor. Product books are quite customarily sponsored, sometimes covertly. I was fortunate, first time of trying, to enlist the co-operation of the global leader in gin. In its upper echelons, the gin trade is less fragmented than the commerce in some other important spirits: internationally, there are few big names, and one dominant brand.

So the association of Gordon's with this work is wholly logical. But this is by no means a company history: there is nothing intrusive in the commercial connection. This is the place to state that opinions, comment, conjectures and prognostications are the author's alone. I have found it pertinent to use aspects of the Tanqueray-Gordon story graphically to illustrate aspects of gin's progress. I would have done so in any circumstances. The company take the broad-minded view that a book, of which the purpose is to increase awareness of gin, can be of benefit to the whole industry: thus it is correct for the industry's leader to initiate such an enterprise.

* * *

I thought long and hard about treatment before I wrote a line. The obvious course was that of straightforward narrative – history, social implications, production, some recipes, the odd anecdote . . . how banal! How boring! So I decided to eliminate commercial statistics for a start, all technical details, sales charts and market share: they are of minimal interest to the consumer, the general reader for whom I am writing. I am not inditing a trade manual. I was aiming at being instructively entertaining. I wanted to evolve a fresh concept in drink books. I came up with the notion of enlivening established facts with imaginary conversations, humanising my story, embellishing the truth by introducing fictional characters alongside real persons, expanding authentic episodes and inventing apt ones, employing pastiche and social satire . . . blending the crafts of historical novelist and of non-fiction author.

That explains the unusual complexion of this book. I could not, of course, let it be just a series of sketches: that would give an incomplete picture. Thus, further to inform, and to give a change of pace, I have annexed to several chapters factual notes and comments, not neglecting apposite digressions. This is a highly individual work, and I have included some personal experiences and other relevant trivia.

* * *

At the conclusion of the book are listed acknowledgements to certain writers and books, some of which are mentioned in the text, that I have found of value or which I recommend.

I am grateful to Mr. Bruce Dehn, Clerk to the Worshipful Company of Distillers, for historical assistance.

I am much indebted to Mrs. Ulla Laing for her contribution (chapter 11) and to the well-known journalist and author Betty James (Mrs. Reeve Jones) for her expert editing of these culinary *chefs-d'oeuvre.*

I wish to express special appreciation to –

Mr. E. W. J. Watkins, whose researches, which he kindly made available to me, were of inestimable value;

Mr. P. J. Tanqueray, who gave me access to archives that threw considerable new light on to gin's story; Mr. R. D. Perry, whose concise precis of gin production, taken from a previous book of mine, cannot be bettered;

Mr R. G. Filby, without whose initial approval my ambition would have been thwarted.

* * *

"Oh, bury me on the lone prairie
Where whiskey's cheap and the gin is free!"
Harry Kovaire (attrib.)

"GIN IS THE PUREST OF ALL SPIRITS . . ."
André Simon.

I know what the great connoisseur meant when he wrote that, for I spoke to him about it. He expressed no particular liking for gin personally, but from his vast experience he recognised that the best gin is produced from the purest distilled alcohol and its subtle flavouring comes from pure botanical sources.

* * *

The craft of distillation long antedates what we call potable spirits. Originally, distillation was a means of concentrating natural essences, to provide fragrant perfumes. (There are the inevitable legends that the Chinese were distilling from rice wine thousands of years ago.) The Moors brought distillation to Western civilisation, when Europe was still largely barbaric. We do not know when it was realised that since alcohol evaporates at a lower temperature than water, by appropriately heating wine an alcoholic vapour is produced which, when cooled, is more

3

spirituous than the original fluid. The first thorough separation of alcohol from wine *(alcool vini)* is thought to have been performed in France around the year 1100. There are references in the late 12th century to some sort of distillation, *uisca beatha* (vernacular for *aqua vitae*), in Ireland. These early distillates must have been rough and weakish alcohol, later known as "low wines". It was three centuries before there is evidence of practical distilling on a commercial scale.

The turning of "low wines" into stronger and purer spirit by further distillation made possible spirits of a purity that rendered them palatable. The Dutch are credited with perfecting secondary distillation, though the principle was known previously to archaic medical science. The production of good spirit on a fairly large scale led directly to gin, the first re-distilled (rectified) and flavoured spirit of any consequence. Gin was later, particularly with the triumph of London Dry gin, to benefit from the invention, in the 1830s, of continuous distillation which can produce very highly rectified – totally pure – spirit that is the foundation of really fine gin.

* * *

The tale of the world's leading spirits is initially one of struggle. They emerged from caverns in hidden glens, from monasteries, from rustic stills in a barely settled continent, evolved from experiments to improve wine shipping, from an intoxicant once used to revive plantations slaves, or derived from so unlikely a source as a brew of tropical vegetation . . .

Unlike most spirits, gin was, from the start, a sound product. We shall see how it changed, became a fashionable, modern drink, why its appeal is so universal, its enjoyment global. Fully to understand the whys and wherefores of gin's success, let us re-wind imaginatively the historical scenario . . .

1

THE NETHERLANDS CONNECTION

1572   A HEALING DRAUGHT

Jacobus was feeling very much better. When he had been admitted into the hospice attached to the Medical Faculty of the University at Leyden he was in miserable condition. The state of the hall where he lay was, by 16th-century standards, excellent. The straw in his palliasse was clean and lice-free, the rushes on the floor harboured no rodents bar the occasional mouse. Nuns, from a neighbouring open order, supplied plain but honest fare. Normally, to be poor and sick and without family was a sad fate. However, the burghers were pious: their charitable impulses had a practical complexion. They were proud to support their celebrated seat of learning and its healing activities. Vaguely, Jacobus realised he was fortunate in his misfortune. Not for him to bother with the great issues of the day – that William of Orange had raised his flag against Spain and the long arm of the Inquisition. His own needs occupied the attention of Jacobus.

Such medications as were received by Jacobus and his indigent companions were herbal. Most of them owed more to superstition than to burgeoning pharmacological science. Jacobus, however, was one of those whose intestinal disorder had been diagnosed by Franciscus de la Böe, who ordered administrating to him doses of his recently perfected elixir. Jacobus did not like its taste, which reinforced his belief that it must be beneficial: its effects were certainly remarkable. By the lift it gave him, he divined the draughts he took three times daily must contain "spirits of wine". Yet this was nothing like the harsh *brandewijn* on which he had sometimes got drunk in periods of comparative affluence.

Once, when one of the acolytes of Professor Sylvius – as de la Böe was familiarly called – was giving Jacobus a measure of his medicine, he had the temerity to enquire that was this potion that made him feel so much easier in his stomach. The answer, that it was *eau de vie de genièvre*, did nothing to satisfy his curiosity, though he was pleased to receive so exotic foreign-sounding a fluid. Within a short time, Jacobus no longer experienced the pains which had sent him pleading for admission, and he was discharged as healed after an examination by the great Professor, Master of the Medical Faculty. The physician pointed at Jacobus as he said to the small group of earnest students, "Do not unhesitatingly ascribe this man's cure to our treatment with genever, for we do not know that nature may herself have done so. We have many more trials to do before we can say that properly purified spirit of grain, compounded with oil of juniper, is positively salubrious and restorative."

Such talk was lost on Jacobus, who gathered his scanty belongings and departed with the nun's blessings ringing in his ears, through which he subconsciously retained the word genever – juniper: for him it held magical connotations.

1574 PIONEER DISTILLER

Jacobus had meandered, with constant stopovers, towards Amsterdam. He was not wholly unskilled and obtained casual work. Lacking dependants, he led an aimless existence, quickly squandering in feeble dissipations the fruits of his occasional industry. Much of the country was in turmoil and Jacobus must live by his wits – which in his case did not make for a high standard of living.

He had a few coins in his pocket when he reached the outskirts of the city. Discovering that there was a small distillery in the neighbourhood, he stopped at its picturesquely sited tap-room, for he was fond of spirits when in funds, if more for their effect than their flavour. When there was any surplus of cereals, particularly spoiled rye which would not make decent bread, these were often turned into cheap forms of *brandewijn*. Though that was not truly "burned [distilled] wine", it was the vernacular for all spirits, which the educated knew as *eaux de vie* and the learned as *aquae vitae*.

Jacobus no longer felt as well as he had two years previously. When he drank rough local distillates, he sometimes thought back to those potent draughts from which he had seemingly so benefited in Leyden. He voiced his memory of them as he sat in that tap-room. A man sitting nearby moved over to his bench. "I work in the distillery here," he said. "I have heard tell of this stuff, and I think my master would be interested to meet one who has drunk it. It might be worth your while if I arrange that you see him." Jacobus had no plans at all, so he readily acquiesced in the proposal.

Thus, the very next day Jacobus stood, cap in hand, before Lucas Bols.

"You say this medicine, or whatever it is, is superior to the spirit we make here?"

"I must admit I do so believe – and better than any I have found elsewhere," said Jacobus, torn between telling the truth and avoiding displeasing this gentleman, whom he knew to be of local influence and who might offer him employment.

"And you think that it healed whatever was wrong with you and also uplifted your whole being?"

"Indeed, sir," answered Jacobus, emboldened by the reception of his opinion, "and I miss it sadly."

"You heard the professor call it genever?"

"Some such word, sir. Also a foreign word."

"That would likely be *genièvre*," said Lucas Bols. "It is French, a language affected by the upper classes."

"I would not know, sir." Jacobus strained his meagre powers of recall, anxious to please.

"There was, sir, mention of pure spirit I think," he said.

"There might well have been." Lucas turned to his foreman. "Pure spirit probably indicates a re-distilling. Alchemists go to such lengths. It could be a costly business. As for juniper, I have thought of it as part of a witches' brew, long on history, short on attraction. But if no less a one than Sylvius of Leyden thinks highly of it, I am interested. Now suppose we were . . ."

Lucas Bols dismissed Jacobus, who, a few guilders the richer, disappears from historical fiction.

"As I was saying before that fellow left, suppose we were to make a concentrated spirit, well re-distilled, and flavour it with juniper." Lucas paused.

"Sir, we are in the business of making spirits for drinking, not medicinal preparations. Juniper is rather bitter. I have heard that in Flanders some Frenchmen have put juniper into spirits of wine but it does not appear to have found favour."

"I know. They must have got it wrong. But if we were to combine the benefits of juniper with refined malt spirit, adding other herbs, and sweeten it – then we might have a palatable distillate with a character hitherto unknown. That illiterate ruffian has given me inspiration! Let us

7

be bold and experiment with formulae. Next year, my new distillery will be operating. What better time than then to launch a novel spirit?"

1585   SOLDIERS OF THE QUEEN

George Farmer was singularly disgusted. He was wet. His helmet, breastplate and pike were rusty. Had he needed to employ it, his arquebus was useless, for his powder was damp. Did it never stop raining in these well-named Low Countries? As usual, rations were short and the countryside bare. October already, and it looked like winter quarters again – and what dismal quarters. A victory of sorts was said lately to have been achieved, at somewhere called Zutphen, but the news was that it had been sorely gained: reportedly, that great gentleman Sir Philip Sidney had died heroically from his wounds.

'Why do we 'ave to fight other folks' wars?" George asked of his sole companion, Bill Cooper, whom he considered something of a fountain of knowledge and who indeed was so in comparison with George.

"Cos it's agin the damned Spaniards. Did you know, our good Bess could 'ave been Queen of the Hollanders? I've been told as 'ow they asked 'er, and she said No, England was enough for 'er, God bless 'er."

"Well I never," said George. "I wish she 'ad accepted, then per'aps bloody Bob Leicester would'nt 'ave been sent over with the likes of us."

They were interrupted by the welcome approach through the mist of a large cart, slowly drawn by two emaciated nags. Though he guessed what it was, abiding by orders, George levelled his worthless firearm and challenged the driver. "Friend," shouted the driver, "and you'll be glad of what we bring."

"So long as it's something to eat," said George.

"That and more." The transport halted, Four guards, who had been sleeping on top of the goods, woke drowsily. With difficulty, they climbed down. Three of them fell to the ground: they were all blind drunk. George and Bill stared at them – with envy. Not a drop of liquor had for many a dank day refreshed the tiny garrison.

A trifle more sober than his colleagues, the driver explained, "We stopped at a still-house on the way, and a rare treat we have for you." He rummaged in the wagon and brought out two stoneware flasks.

"We can do with some Dutch Courage," said Bill, "even if it be that rot-gut they call brandywine."

"You're in for a surprise," said the driver. "Have you any money?"

"When did you last see any pay?" said Bill. "You will 'ave to trust us."

"Well, seeing as how I didn't exactly buy this – rules of war – I can afford to treat you," said the driver, breaking the seal on a flask. "This is no ordinary stuff I can tell you."

They moved the supine guards near enough to the brazier to stop them freezing: they snored on. The driver took a swig from the flask and passed it to George who did likewise before handing it to Bill.

George felt the ardent spirit spread a glow through his entire body: a delicious fragrance delighted his nostrils. Ignorant of poetry, he did not know what was implied by the word nectar or he would so have described this liquid.

"What's in it?" he asked. "I've never tested the like. Do the Hollanders 'ave a name for it?"

"When we was – er, what you might call bargaining for it, I did hear repeated 'ginavver' or summat of that sort. One of 'em who spoke a bit of English said not to take 'is 'ginnavver' it sounded like."

"Ginavver," repeated George. "What's that signify?"

"Does it matter. My time's up soon and when I gets out I'm going to be sure and take some of this 'ome with me."

"You mean *if* you gets out," said George.

"There's a city called Ginever," put in Bill, the unit's intellectual.

"What, in this country?" asked the driver.
"I don't think so," said Bill.
"Then why the devil call it ginavver?"
"I don't know, nor care," said George. "Pass the flask."

NOTES:

1572 A HEALING DRAUGHT

Though he did not, of course, commercialise gin, Sylvius of Leyden is generally accepted as the product's progenitor. It seems probable that juniper-flavoured distillates were first made in some form in Flanders, on France's northern borders, in the 1560s by Hugenot refugees. That must have been very rough: Sylvius perfected it.

1574 PIONEER DISTILLER

Lucas Bols is credited with being the original commercial distiller of gin (not yet so called). In fact, no one knows who was. But the firm of Bols (now a giant of the drinks trade, making many spirits and liqueurs and holding important agencies) is the senior of world-famous distillers still extant. Therefore, I have used Lucas broadly to illustrate a phase in gin's early development from medicine to social beverage.

1585 SOLDIERS OF THE QUEEN

Awareness of gin (geneva) by the English has been attributed to earlier and to later factors.

Marlborough's soldiers had a strong influence in bringing to England continental spirits, but they were certainly not the first. Traders and seafarers also played their part. Netherlands sources inform me that the campaign in which I set my little tale was crucial in familiarising Englishmen with gin.

* * *

Genever, jenever, Geneva all feature in early references to the spirit. Schiedam did not become an important distilling centre, and an alternative name for gin, until the 17th century, when Hollands also became a synonym. As to the contraction to Gin, it is by most accepted that it was by a typically English linguistic distortion. The only minority theory is that it derives from *ginepro* or *ginevra:* Italian (juniper). Switzerland's Geneva has nothing to do with it, though it is a coincidence that several early distillers were Calvinists, whose spiritual leader was a native of Geneva. Some Spanish-speaking countries call gin Ginebra, their word for the city, thus perpetuating a fallacy.

* * *

The first instructions for making "gin" *(Aqua Juniperi)* were published in Amsterdam in 1622.

* * *

"Don't tell my mother I'm living in sin,
Don't let the old folks know;
Don't tell my twin that I breakfast on gin,
He'd never survive the blow."

A. P. Herbert

2

ENGLAND'S WELCOME

1653   "THE DISTILLER OF LONDON"

After the establishment of the Commonwealth in England in 1649, Sir Theodore de Mayerne-Turquet virtually retired to his home in the village of Chelsea. However, he maintained close contact with the Worshipful Company of Distillers, of the City of London, of which he was Perpetual Principal Assistant. He had founded that institution when he was physician to the late Charles I, in conjunction with his friend, Thomas Cademan, the Queen's doctor, who became first master of the Company. From the King, Sir Theodore had obtained, in 1638, a Royal Charter which conferred extensive powers on the Company of Distillers, covering the Cities of London and Westminster and to a surrounding distance of twenty-one miles. Within the area, the rules of the Company regulated the activities of all distillers: that included makers of spirituous medicines, "strong waters" [spirits], and also vinegars (then as much made from beer and ale as from wine). Yet, despite, or because of, Royal support, the City – which was Parliamentarian in complexion – refused the Distillers recognition, and did not do so until 1672.

Sir Theodore and Thomas Cademan incorporated the Charter of the Company with a long list of recipes, which was published as "The Distiller of London." It was a tribute to the esteem in which Sir Theodore was held that, following the King's execution, the Charter was not abrogated. The powers of the Company were reinforced by the 1652 edition of "The Distiller of London": it ensured the Distillers' right to exact penalties for infringement of their rules "under the Laws of the Commonwealth".

The significance of Sir Theodore in our story lies in his insistence on

11

rectification of spirits. Rectification (purification) was vital to the emergence of good gin. Though production of geneva (gin) in England was still in its infancy in Sir Theodore's day – it is not specifically mentioned in his book – within forty years the better London gin distillers would be using properly rectified spirit.

The Distillers' Company prohibited the sale of "low spirits". They must be turned into "strong proof spirit, whereby they may be corrected and cured of their natural, harsh, distasteful, unsavoury or evil qualities, before they be compounded with ingredients". Gin is the premier rectified spirit compounded with ingredients. What Sir Theodore called "low spirits" are now universally known as "low wines". These are the product of the first distillation from traditional pot-stills. "Low wines" can be rectified, and strengthened, by re-distillation, several times if necessary, as Sir Theodore realised. With the invention of continuous distillation, in the 1830s, gin distillers had access to even more highly rectified spirit. See also Chapter 6.

1663 MR. PEPYS CURES THE COLLYWOBBLES

On 7th October, Samuel Pepys was feeling decidedly under the weather. The previous day he had entertained a relative and friends at home, without prior arrangement, and, having no suitable victuals in the house, he sent out for dishes from a local cookhouse. He was upset that his servants were so neglectful that they did not transpose the food but served it at table in bowls clearly marked with the cook's name. He feared that his guest, as he wrote in his diary, "if they observed anything, they might know it was not my own dinner".

He had further reason for wishing he had stuck to home-cooked viands, for on the next two days he had to record that he suffered from "My great fit of cholic." On the 10th "Sir J. Minnes and Sir W. Batten did advise me to take some juniper wine: strong water [spirit] made with Juniper." This put his stomach to rights: on the following day, Sunday, he was his usual self.

1690 A BREWER TEMPTED

John Bristow sat in his brew-house, attached to the Four Peacocks Tavern. John was renowned for his beer. With him, watching the casks being filled and rolled away for ripening, was Silas Bugg. The establishment was the most favoured in the parish: it had lately been refurbished, following its reconstruction, for its precursor had gone up in flames during the Great

Fire of London fourteen years earlier: John Bristow's father had never fully recovered from his experiences in that disaster.

"Under the recent Act of Parliament, under our glorious sovereigns," said Silas, who until two years ago had been vociferous in his loyalty to the deposed James the Second, "I may distil as much spirits as I care to or that my apparatus will allow of. Can you not sell some for me to our mutual profit? That is what I am asking."

"Reckon I could," answered John, "for to be sure, the importation of the Frenchies' brandy has been stopped. I hear it remains in goodly supply on the Southern coast where the smugglers have the better of the Revenue, but not a drop have I been offered this twelvemonth that I could afford or dared buy. You'll be making this Hollands I suppose. Do you think folk will really take to it?"

"Indeed they will, for it is not the least costly. Already Hollands, or Geneva as it is more usually called, is much drunk in Portsmouth, in Bristol and particularly in Plymouth I hear. Some is as good as that of the Dutch themselves. A man I know in Portsmouth is making thirty gallons of Hollands a day and could sell more if he could extend his factory."

"Does not the Company of Distillers hold a monopoly in our City and that of Westminster?" queried John, who, despite his profession, was basically an honest and law-abiding man, though anxious to purvey anything profitable.

"Against the new Act the Distillers are powerless," said Silas. "I ran foul of them three years ago but now I can thumb my nose at them. Production of spirit is almost our patriotic duty, for it gives encouragement to the farmers by allowing them a new market for their corn."

"You make your spirits from wheat? I use only costly barley for my brews."

"From wheat or rye or oats, even when spoiled. Any of them can ferment and be distilled. My greatest expense is for juniper berries and herbs and sugar, though I sometimes dispense with them – though not for proper Geneva such as I propose to you," Silas added.

This caused John Bristow to consider, since he could easily make an alcoholic wash in his brew-house, which he might himself distil, as anyone was permitted to do under the new laws. All he needed was the equipment and some expertise in how to turn this into Geneva. For the moment, though, he would buy from Silas and see how this ardent liquor appealed to his customers.

"I will take a trial cask from you, Silas, I shall pay for as much as I may sell and you will take back any I may not."

"Very well – you shall have a hogshead."

"A barrel will suffice for a start," said the cautious John.

"A barrel of some thirty-six gallons then. It will be proven spirit. You may sell it as such, or break it down with water which will increase your profits."

"Water my goods!" exclaimed John, who could afford not to indulge in such dilution, common enough despite the efforts of the ale conners of the Brewers Company.

"That is up to you," said Silas. "There are, in effect, no regulations, though doubt not that should the distilling trade prosper Parliament will find a means to tax us."

1692   AN EXPANDING COMMERCE

J ohn Bristow did not waste much time. He had substantially expanded his brew-house and was capable of making large quantities of "beer" from which to distil, buying whatever cereals were cheapest. With two alembics – primitive but effective stills – and a little expert advice, he was able to keep up a more or less continuous production of rough alcohol. From Silas Burg, with whom he was no longer on friendly terms, he had learned, by flattery and bribery of his foreman, how to compound his spirit with juniper, sugar and aromatics he bought from an apothecary, or rather exchanged for Geneva which the latter sold – for medicinal use, of course. For the medical origins of the product had become quite widely recognised.

In the much enlarged bar of the Four Peacocks, behind the curving counter were now four tall casks, labelled "Bristow's Finest Geneva", "Bristow's Old Special", "Bristow's Famous Comforter", and "Glorious Revolution Nectar". The last was a reminder of the political turmoil of which one result had been the freeing of distillation that had so added to John's prosperity. Each cask contained identical spirit, the difference being that the first-named was close to proof spirit. The others were progressively diluted, "Glorious Revolution" being the weakest and cheapest. So a man could drink more of it, and spend more, before having had enough or prior to falling into a stupour or becoming rowdy and attracting the unwanted attention of the Watch.

* * *

"Do you know," said John Bristow to Alderman Jones, for he had a very mixed clientele, "last month I sold almost as much gallonage of Geneva as of beer? One can scarcely credit so great a change in so short a time."

"I dare say," remarked the Alderman, drawing on a clay churchwarden pipe that John had himself filled with choice Virginian tobacco in respect for his most distinguished customer, "I dare say you speak the truth." They were sitting in the snug parlour, removed from the ordinary rabble. "I would never myself have touched Geneva had it not been for the example of our royal master. I have it on the highest authority that King William sets great store by Hollands, as it is usually called out of regard for His Majesty, and it is regularly served at Hampton Court. A sheriff of my acquaintance – you will bear with me if I do not name him – attended a levée and heard from one of the courtiers that the royal residence is irreverently referred to as 'the gin temple'."

"Gin temple," repeated John, impressed by a revelation from so elevated a social source. "I suppose gin is a shortened form of Geneva."

"That must indeed be the case. Gin is the latest word for it though it has yet to pass into the vulgar speech."

John made a mental note to change the lettering on some of his casks: how would "Bristow's Gin Royal" look?

"Unfortunately," continued Jones, accepting another glass and pretending to pay as John waved his hand away with a smile. "Unfortunately, Geneva is tending to become too much liked by the labouring class. In disreputable ale-houses, which should not sell ardent liquor and are frequently unlicensed, rank spirits purporting to pass for Geneva are being drunk by toss-pots and ruffians with a dishonest penny or so in their pockets. Such places are the resorts of thieves and harlots and seduce shiftless workers into idleness and debauchery. They bring, through reflected disgrace, a bad complexion to such excellent establishments as are owned by merchants of your calibre." John smirked sycophantically. "The City fathers are unable to control these growing abuses. Good money is being expended on cheap spirits that should be supporting families, until it be all gone, and women and children, lacking bread, became a burden on their parishes."

"I have heard rumour of such happenings," said John, who supplied untreated plain spirit to two disreputable places. Perhaps he should be more careful.

"My Lord Mayor himself has expressed in my hearing some alarm that the unfettered manufacture and sale of strong spirits may finally lead to public disorder and he may feel obliged to ask Parliament to intervene." John Bristow felt uneasy at once: it was precisely this unfettered distillation that was enriching him.

"Any pestilential blots on the fair face of the city must be obliterated," he said with feigned indignation, wishing to stay in well with his companion. "Cannot the Court of Common Council close these felonious liquor shops?"

"We feel it is becoming a matter for the government," said the alderman, ready as any civic dignitary to shift responsibility. "However, there are powerful interests involved, especially the agricultural magnates who greatly profit by the sale of grain for distillers' use. And there is the King himself, who might not look kindly on action seemingly aimed against the celebrated product that originated in his native land."

"Yet any repression would surely fall on to the lawbreakers, not honest distillers," insisted John.

"Often the innocent suffer in the correction of wrongs perpetrated by the guilty," said the alderman sententiously. John did not much care for the way the conversation was going: did the alderman know more than he was telling? Was some curtailment of distilling being seriously bruited in governing circles? But Parliament usually moved lethargically: there was probably little real cause for concern.

"Do you think 'Bristow's Gin Royal' would be a suitable name for one of my Genevas? I would admire your advice," he said.

The alderman emptied his glass and put it down with a sigh of approval.

"An excellent liquor," he opined. "Yes, I think your title a splendid one for your best Geneva." With a faintly malicious grin, he added, "But do not water it excessively."

1738   THE CAPTAIN MAKES A KILLING

Initially, the Act of Parliament of 1736, which virtually outlawed gin, was a gift to Captain Dudley Bradstreet, very much a man of his times and none too particular how he earned his livelihood. Most established distillers, of which there were hundreds, went out of business or became moonshiners overnight. Bootleggers (a term not to gain currency for another 150 years) proliferated and illegal drinking dens sprang up like fungi on the metropolitan scene.

Informants against lawbreakers were paid a handsome ten pounds – by the person informed on, who, in default, faced jail for two months plus a whipping. This seemed easy pickings for Dudley, but it was money dangerously earned. Several of his acquaintances in the same line disappeared mysteriously or were found murdered in gruesome circumstances. Not infrequently were informers' corpses recovered by Thames boatmen. Nor were the Courts too ready to believe an informer's word, in which case emnity was incurred without any concomitant reward, and the danger of revenge enhanced.

Being more ingenious than courageous, Dudley several times narrowly escaped the fury of a gin-inspired – or gin-deprived – mob. He came to an abrupt decision: he would switch camps. It was apparent that, such was the insatiable thirst for gin amongst the populace, there was more gain, and less risk, on the wrong side of the law. Though acquainted with the Act in question, he now studied it from a different angle, and discovered an

interesting loophole. He was well aware that an informer must know the name of the owner of rented property from which gin was illegally sold. It was an omission in law that intrigued him. It gave the magistrates no powers to break into suspected premises in order to arrest malefactors.

So Dudley acquired access to a house, the exact ownership of which it would be difficult to prove. He firmly secured it against forcible entry and moved in with a supply of durable provisions, foreseeing a long stay in his little fortress. Next purchase was a lead pipe and a trade sign depicting a cat. One end of the pipe was fixed under the cat's paw, where there was also a slot: at the other end, inside the house, was a small funnel. The place had a well-hidden back entrance. To this was duly delivered a quantity of gin from

Mr. Langdale's distillery in Holborn. This cost him £13, leaving him with but two shillings in ready money. It was, by the standards of the day, good gin, and the distiller was aware unofficially of the enterprise from which he hoped to gain custom in hard times for legal distilling.

All that was now required was some publicity. Dudley let it be known by word of mouth that gin could from the following day be obtained – from a cat. This animal would be found in Blue Anchor Alley in St. Luke's parish.

Dudley suffered anxious hours the next morning. He had risen early and the time seemed interminable before, as he was later to record: "At last I heard the chink of money, and a comfortable voice say, 'Puss, give me two pennyworth of gin.' I instantly put my mouth to the tube and bid them receive it from the pipe under her paw, and then measured and poured into the funnel, from whence they soon received it."

By nightfall, Dudley had gained six shillings. News of this pioneering "coin-op" retail outlet, so greatly to the public taste, quickly spread: there was still a dearth of spots where gin could be bought in small quantities. On the second day, Dudley's takings were thirty shillings and continued to rise: in his first month he got £22, comfortably covering his investment. He saw riches ahead.

"From all parts of London," he was to recall, "people used to resort to me in such numbers that my neighbours could scarcely get in or out of their houses." Later: "The street now became quite impassable by the numbers who came out of curiosity to see the (sic) Inchanted Cat, for so Puss was called. This concourse of idle people had such an effect that my neighbours went to their several landlords and declared their houses were not tenable unless they got the Cat-man removed. They [the landlords] asked who the Cat-man was, but received no other information than that he was the greatest nuisance they ever saw or heard of."

Dudley's subterfuge was working. He moved his attractive girl friend into the house (through that hidden back entry?) and she was gratified by the money that was pouring in. But all this could not indefinitely escape attention from the civic authorities. One day a gaggle of magistrates, with their constables, laid seige to the Cat's house, attended by a large throng of onlookers and potential customers who were furious at being barred from the famous tube. Knocks on the barricaded door brought answer, but not admittance, by Dudley. Knowing the officers had no right of entry, he prevailed upon his lady-love to go upstairs and address the assembly from a window. Agreeing, she put on her best finery, and, being a woman of beauty and wit, quickly entranced her audience, a large proportion of whom, one suspects, were intoxicated – including, a view of the period, some of the officials. Primed by Dudley, she told them:

"If you have lawful authority to break open my doors, spare them not: otherwise, at your peril be it." We may presume a certain poetic licence in Dudley's record of her speech. She continued, "My manners are very inoffensive. Here my cat and I sell only the water of life, which if drunk by any persons they shall never die while they continue using it."

So overcome by this harangue, according to Dudley, were five auditors that "they instantly threw themselves on their knees to worship her. The justices and other officers begged her pardon and sneaked off, being hooted by the insulting mob."

Allowing for some hyperbole on Dudley's part, the fact is that he was not arrested. He continued in business for another three months, amassing a small fortune. Yet, as happens to many commercial pioneers, his ideas were copied. So many imitators arrived with their own dispensers, and illicit sellers multiplied, that Dudley retired from the gin trade and thus from our story.

1749 THE POWER OF A PICTURE

William Hogarth had long left behind him his humble, though comfortable, origins. His portraits earned money, and he reached a wider public through engravings of moralistic and satiric pictures which combined observation on low life with comment on the vices of the upper classes. His popular "Strolling Actresses Dressing In A Barn", illustrating the hardships of ordinary theatre people at that time, had a hint of salaciousness and included a young man being plied with gin – medicinally some (but not all) commentators suggested.

William, no Puritan although a critic of excesses, knew about the grim intoxication of London proletariat, with thousands daily sodden on "Parliamentary Brandy", as Cockney wit described unflavoured distillates made to evade laws designed to curb the trade in gin. He took a general insobriety for granted, even a source of comic inspiration, for it was a commonplace for a judge to sit drunk in Court as he sentenced a felon to death. No one thought the worse of a Member of Parliament if he were to make a speech under the manifest influence of liquor – nor indeed if he were too inebriated to do more than snore on his bench.

Yet there was something about this addiction to strong drink that offended William's artistic sensibilities and his social conscience which was better developed than that of most of his contemporaries. He had satirised the boozing gentry in his "A Modern Midnight Conversation". In his mind, William considered how he might bring his particular talents to support the interests of his less fortunate compatriots. A theme came to him when, with

friends, he stopped during an outing on horseback to Highgate, a pleasant village in the hills to the north of London. Amongst a mixed crowd at the inn at which they had paused was a party of respectable workingmen who were spending on convivial tots of gin the wages of their toil. From amicable banter, as the quarterns of spirit were emptied, they passed to an exchange of insults, to swearing for real and then to fisticuffs, with the results that one man laid another unconscious with a blow from a pewter tankard.

William had witnessed many a fight in his urban excursions: it was not uncommon for even aristocrats to brawl in the streets and fracas in taverns were part of everyday life, often involving women, too, for that matter. But somehow this particular scene in Highgate, a peaceful semi-rural spot, touched William deeply. Back in his studio, he broadened and transposed his inspiration, which must have been resting in his mind awaiting a catalyst. He started to create on canvas a savage, crowded scene of total civic debauchery and decay, an epitome of intemperance. He called it "Gin Lane."

NOTES

1652 "THE DISTILLER OF LONDON"

The particular edition (there were several) of this important book is curious in that, published a year before Cromwell assumed supreme power as Lord Protector, its preface incorporated King Charles's Charter, replete with regal arms and royal references. Its full title was: "The Distiller of London: with the Clavis [keys] to unlock the deepest Secrets of the Mysterious Art. With many additions to the Most Excellent Cordial Waters which have been pen'd by our most able Doctors and Physicians, Ancient and Modern, Foreign and Domestick. Now published for the Publike good."

Sir Theodore de Mayerne was a remarkable man. Born in Geneva, he showed early brilliance and as a young man became physician to Henry IV of France. Before that monarch's assassination, he migrated to England and became doctor to James I, who knighted him. Apart from his appointment under Charles I, he is credited with being physician to Charles II, making a record of service to four sovereigns – but he did not follow Charles into exile and died in 1655, five years before the Restoration. Sir Theodore succumbed, aged 82, allegedly as a result of drinking infected wine in a London tavern, sad fate for a distiller. He was a renowned gourmet and a cookery book by him was published posthumously.

Sir Theodore might be dubbed the father of English distilling and thus, by inference, of English gin as well. His influence in promoting fine distilling was eventually profound. Had the rules of his Company been enforced, had the City authorities been more supportive, some of the tribulations of the next century's Gin Era could have been avoided.

1663 MR. PEPYS CURES THE COLLYWOBBLES

The extract from the famous Diary indicates that, so far as the affluent in England were concerned, "Gin" was then a medicinal item. His "strong water made with Juniper" exactly describes old Geneva.

1690 A BREWER TEMPTED

It was the "glorious revolution" of 1688 that marked the real welcoming of gin by the English. James II was deposed and the monarchial gap was filled by inviting William (son of the famous Prince of Orange and grandson of Charles I) to become co-sovereign with his Stuart consort, Mary (eldest daughter of the rejected James). If plenty of citizens remembered that twenty years previously ships from William's homeland had sailed up the lower Thames and set fire to English naval vessels at Chatham, that was conveniently forgotten by the majority.

William and Mary were violently hostile to France, albeit the latter's father was the guest of Louis XIV at Versailles.

The Act of Parliament referred to, passed early in the new reign, was backed by the powerful influence of the big landowners who had supported King William's candidature. It was aimed at aiding "distillation of brandy and spirits from corn. First, the trade and commerce of France being prohibited and all their goods from being imported into this Kingdom; and whereas good and whole-some Brandy, aquae vitae and spirits may be made from corn; for the encouragement therefore of making of Brandy, strong waters and spirits from malted corn, and for the greater consumption of corn and the advantage of tillage in this Kingdom, the King, the Queen and the Parliament assembled have thus ordained . . . [that virtually anyone has the right to distil.]" Brandy was then a synonym for any distilled spirits: the additional descriptions are legalistic tautology. Corn embraced most cereal crops, but mainly referred to wheat of which England then, bar the occasional poor harvest, usually had a surplus.

1692 AN EXPANDING COMMERCE

Though the Distiller's Company's control of the trade was not officially abolished by the 1689 Act, it was effectively negated. Why was it to gin to which the embryonic distilling industry turned? Not just for the King's natal connection to be sure. It was because it was the only spirit of the manufacture of which there was any native experience – and there existed already a small demand. Scottish and Irish distillations were unknown to the general English public, though soldiers and hardy travellers had encountered "wusky". There lacked wine to turn into grape brandy. Cider was a traditional local English drink and also enjoyed vogue in higher circles: it was relished by Charles II. Though there once was a little-known distillate from it called "Cider Royal", and earlier than the 17th century colonists in North America were making applejack brandy, distillation from cider never caught on in England: perhaps there was not enough or it was too costly a base for spirits. So gin it had to be.

The word Gin is first recorded in writing in 1714: I have assumed its colloquial use somewhat earlier.

1738 THE CAPTAIN MAKES A KILLING

This true tale, allowing for exaggerations, is re-told from Bradstreet's autobiographical *Life and Uncommon Adventures* (1754), written in his prosperous retirement. It serves to epitomise the situation after the 1736 Act and the inability of the authorities to enforce its well-meaning but idiotic requirements.

1749 THE POWER OF A PICTURE

I have fleshed out the widely accepted story of Hogarth's inspiration for his famous picture. Its influence was remarkable. The brutal impact of *Gin Lane* had a bad effect on the reputation, not the popularity, of gin for a long time. As a comment on low life in the mid-18th century, *Gin Lane* remains a masterpiece. It has survived: and so has gin.

On referring to two late 19th century books, although that was a period prolific in anti-drink movements, in their biographies of William Hogarth neither volume mentions *Gin Lane* amongst lists of his major works.

BACKGROUND TO THE "GIN ERA"

RESUMÉ OF LEGISLATION FROM CONCLUSION OF 17TH CENTURY TO END OF 18TH

1690 – English distilling given almost total freedom and production of spirits (gin) actively encouraged by government.

1694 – Beer taxes raised, so gin in many instances actually cheaper than brews. Taste for gin acquired by folk who might otherwise not have taken to it.

1702 – Queen Anne ascends to throne. She revokes Charter of Distillers Company, abolishing their residual powers to curb poor distillations.

1720 – Mutiny Act absolves tradesmen of any sort who are distillers from having soldiers billetted on them. As these are mostly very unwelcome guests, many more innkeepers and others turn to making gin.

1721 – Justices of the Peace in City of Westminster complain that deplorable situation has arisen where one in ten houses within their jurisdiction sell gin. Unofficial figures give it as one in four.

1727 – National (mainly London) distillation of gin rises to 5 million gallons (22m litres).

1729 – First of the "Gin Acts". Distillers to take out licenses for £20 (a large amount at the time) and pay excise tax of 2 shillings a gallon. "Compounded spirit" (meaning gin) specifically mentioned. Thus, legitimate distillers and retailers penalised. Unflavoured base spirit escapes law and becomes known as Parliamentary Brandy. Illicit distilling thrives.

1733 – Despite taxation, in London alone quantity of gin distilled rises to 11 million gallons (50m litres). This does not include huge amounts illegally produced or on which tax evaded. Act of 1729 repealed. It is replaced by laws reducing ease with which gin can be sold – i.e. not by street hawkers from barrows, nor ordinary shops. Intentions not achieved as spirits may only be sold from a residence: this inept piece of legislation turns every house into a potential tavern.

1736 – In reply to representations, House of Commons resolves that sale of spirits should be confined to conventional retailers such as taverns, licensed dram shops, coffee houses; also by doctors and apothecaries "for medicinal use". However, the Act passed implementing these suggestions is much more drastic. It lays down that spirits may not be sold in lesser quantities than 2 gallons, puts the retail license at a prohibitive £50 annually and imposes tax of £1 a gallon. Only three distillers (until 1743) consider it worth staying in business. Illicit sale flourishes (*see* – The Captain Makes a Killing, *1738*).

1742 – Ridiculously ineffective 1736 Act is repealed.

1743 – A further "Gin Act" endeavours more sensibly to control sale and public consumption of strong liquor. Licences of £1 to be paid by existing holders of beer and ale licences. Distillers not to retail gin but only sell to licensed houses. London produces nearly 20 million gallons of gin (91m litres), which is mostly sold in the capital – population 500,000. Insobriety the order of the day. Inebriated ruling class deplores intoxication of the masses.

1747 – Distillers petition Parliament to be allowed to sell direct to consumers. Permission given with £50 license. Consumption of gin rises – so beer tax reduced as counter-measure. It does not much affect the situation.

1750 – Publication of Hogarth's *Gin Lane*. See *1749*.

1751 – Henry Fielding, author of *Tom Jones* and respected Bow Street magistrate, publishes influential pamphlet linking cheap gin with major rise in petty crime – which carries far from petty penalties. Yet a further "Gin Act" passed, giving more teeth to that of 1743. Much to distress of their custodians, jails and workhouses forbidden to sell gin to inmates. Sale of gin by chandlers prohibited. (Chandlers, originally candle-makers, in 18th century sold provisions, coal and daily necessities, largely to the poor. Some chandlers had set up as distillers.) Only fairly substantial publicans allowed to sell gin: if they allow credit to customers, no sum under £1 recoverable in law.

1756 – Improvement made to 1751 Act.

1757 – Marked improvement in regulation of gin trade favourably commented on by James Hanway, the sociologist (a term mercifully not yet invented). Bad harvest – repeated in 1759–60 – brings periodic prohibition on use of corn for distilling. Gin becomes more expensive and this adds to its respectability – but not much.

1780 – Anti-Catholic riots in London on horrendous scale, stirred up by fanatical Lord George Gordon. Mob sacks many Catholic-owned premises, including Langdale's distillery – supplier to Captain Dudley Bradstreet (q.v.).

1791 – Minor extra curtailments in legal outlets for gin. Excise tax reaches point where gin – legally made and sold – becomes temporarily beyond reach of labouring classes.

The "Gin Era" draws to a conclusion. England has truly welcomed gin: it is an ineluctable aspect of social life. It can now start its slow climb to social *acceptance*.

* * *

"Gin! Gin! a drop of Gin
When, darkly, Adversity's days set in . . ."   *Thomas Hood (1799–1845)*

3

THE TRIUMPH OF LONDON

1822   RISE OF A GREAT COMPANY

Report by Joseph Ambrose, antiquarian and local historian, of St. Bride's Lane in the City of London. Taken down by him, in Mavor's system of stenography, at the residence of Alexander Gordon, Esqre, Distiller. Discovered amongst Mr. Ambrose's papers after his demise, and presumably part of an uncompleted larger work on City institutions.

"I had requested an appointment with Mr. Gordon, on account of his eminent position and in pursuance of certain enquiries I have been making into London's growing importance in the production of Schiedam, Geneva, Hollands, or what we now more usually call Gin. I wished to record for posterity some history of this individual who has witnessed fundamentary changes in the product with which his name is indelibly connected. He is now eighty years of age.

"Mr. Gordon graciously received me in the library of his fine mansion in Charterhouse Square. He had beside him on a table a beautiful decanter of Bristol blue glass, gilded with the title 'Hollands'. I surmised this was gin from his patronymic establishment and was not displayed for effect, though I declined his offer of some, it not yet being eleven o'clock of the morning. My host poured for himself. He added some liquid and dropped in a little hot water from a silver pot. "It being raw without," he explained, "I take gin with essence of cloves, which I find a prime specific against chills." Mr. Gordon's robust appearance at his advanced years is indeed a tribute to his regime.

"I now give the gist of his conversation with me, in his own words, with my interpolations and queries omitted in the interests of fluency."

MR. GORDON'S STATEMENT:

My father, George Gordon, was said to have left Scotland after the troubles of '15. I do not know the truth of this for he rarely spoke of his time north of the Border and, like many of his countrymen he was an Englishman by adoption though proud of his lineage. He became a merchant. However, from his native country he brought some knowledge of distilling – where acquired I cannot say – and took part in the gin trade, then in its infancy and none too reputable.

I was born in Wapping, on the north side of the Thames, with the south banks of which I was destined to have close association. Before that, on my father's death, when I was not yet four years old, I was sent to my grandfather's home. He also was Alexander and lived in Glasgow. Why I went, or with whom I journeyed, I have no notion. The tone of my sojourn was set the very first evening. Before me was put as my supper a dish of porridge oats. Though by ancestry a Scot, I had never seen the stuff before. I refused it and was sent to bed unfed. At breakfast the next morning, the same dish was placed in front of me and again I refused it. However, by dinner-time hunger overcame distaste and pride, and I ate the lot.

The following years are of no import. Suffice it to say that as soon as might be I travelled South, accompanied by a cadet of the Sandeman clan whose kinsman, John, was later to succeed well for himself and his family in the Spanish trade.

After transactions of little public consequence, in 1769 I married my cousin, Susannah Herbert. From that happy event I date the foundation of Gordon & Company, about which you have been good enough to enquire.

We lived from the start in this house where we are now talking. It has a superior environment to that of Bermondsey, in the diocese of Southwark, south of the river, where I maintained a family connection with a spirit rectifying plant until as late as '93. As an historian you will be aware that earlier in Southwark, outside the jurisidiction of the City, was a notorious grog-shop that we are told displayed the sign – "Drunk for a penny, dead drunk for tuppence, clean straw for nothing". The topers could sleep off their intoxication on the very premises that caused it. That was in the bad old days, before the trade was put on a proper footing and before the Gordons were involved in it, yet I find it entertaining to think that we were making fine spirit close to where a couple of generations previous they had sold rot-gut masquerading as gin.

I became discontented with the salubrity of Bermondsey. The water comes much from marshland and it was none too easy of access – until Mr. Rennie's Southwark Bridge was opened three years ago. Though rectification is a process of purification so far as spirit be concerned, I looked for a cleaner source of water in the compounding of our gin. The answer lay on my doorstep, for Charterhouse Square lies close on the borders of Clerkenwell, which is beyond the polluted soil of the City proper and is rich in springs. My friend, neighbour and competitor, Sheriff Booth of Turnmill Street, has good supplies from his own well. In the middle of the last century, Sam Whitbread came to Clerkenwell to use its water for his brews. I expect you have taken the medicinal waters at Dr. Sadler's wells. Initially, I found what I required in the vicinity of nearby St. John's Street, at Corporation Row. Shortly before my retirement I moved the business to larger premises a short distance away in Goswell Street. I believe that name may derive from God's Well. Yes, as you say, another theory is from Goose or Gosling Well, possibly a reference to the farms now disappeared from the district. Because of its great production of alcoholic beverages, not only gin, Clerkenwell was a prime target for the mob during the so-called Gordon Riots – that description caused some wry smiles afterwards – but, as did Mr. Booth, I armed my senior employees with muskets as troubles loomed, and my watchmen with fearsome cudgels, and we kept the rioters at bay.

What was formerly simply Gordon & Company now has the rather cumbersome title of Gordon Knight, Son and Brigg – and you have asked my why that is so. I will tell you the following for your private information and on your word that you will not publish it within my lifetime. Earlier, I had one Foote as a partner, which proved unsatisfactory. In William Knight I discovered a valued and loyal servant, doing much to disseminate appreciation of our wares. He was helpful in ridding us of Foote. For this and his other attributes he became a partner. Briggs is Knight's son-in-law, his promotion being an item of nepotism I might have vetoed had I been more active in the company's affairs at the time. I cannot really bother myself with comparatively trivial matters. They are of no import to me so long as Gordon & Company – as I continue to call it – expand sales and profits.

Myself an only child, I was blessed with ten children. My eldest son shows no inclination to matrimony, and my second-born, Charles, who resides in Goswell Street, has demonstrated no great interest in commerce. However, he has a son, another Charles Gordon, and thus the succession – if I do not use too grand a word – seems assured. I have numerous other grand-children.

I have seen enormous changes in our trade. It has to be noticed that gentlemen in the City are not infrequently to be seen drinking gin, with aromatics, and no longer leaving it to their womenfolk. I have heard say that Lord Byron likes gin, though whether, coming from such a man that is a recommendation, I am not sure. Yet I dare say some young bucks may follow his example.

A development I would care to see would be for leading distillers increasingly to put their gins in their own crocks or bottles, on which it would of course be necessary to charge a returnable fee in view of the cost of such containers. These vessels would come back to the proprietors for re-filling with their own product. Often now, our casks, displayed in tap-rooms and carrying our name boldly, do not only contain our gin but are diluted with baser spirit or wholly filled with substitutes, to the detriment of our trade and reputation and to the deception of the public. There remain a few malpractices by minor distilleries, yet the whole tone of our trade has immeasurably improved in my lifetime and I am sanguine as to its future. Gin is no longer confined to the great cities: it is universally used in England, thanks largely to the canals. Quite small communities may as easily enjoy it as the inhabitants of, say, Bristol. Speaking of that part of the country, I recently received a letter from an old acquaintance, the Rev. John Skinner, with whom you may be aware from his antiquarian researches. He holds a living outside Bath and he tells me that the villagers are much given to gin-drinking. Perhaps I should rather say that he complains, for his parishioners seem to be a drunken lot. I have not yet replied to him, being torn between satisfaction at extension of business and abhorrence of intemperance!

What has greatly pleased me is the dominance of London in our trade and, if I may say so, I take deep satisfaction for the modest role I have played in this success. Outside of Plymouth and Warrington, I cannot think of any city with a major distillery. London and its immediate environs has virtually the entire gin trade of this country: I think we may say with pride that we have comfortably outstripped Holland, the home of gin. But we produce almost entirely for domestic consumption. There are great possibilities, as yet scarcely exploited, for sales overseas, particularly in our colonies. Gin is highly suitable to torrid climes, where local liquors are of dubious quality. However, the government has remained obdurate to our entreaties to be relieved of duty on gin when it is exported, whereby our commerce might be considerably enlarged to the eventual benefit of the Treasury.

And now I would be glad if you would join me in a dram, as my grandfather – of whom I recall little else – used to say when proferring the peaty spirit of his homeland.

* * *

"I now willingly took of some gin, Mr. Gordon having called a servitor to replenish the hot water, and we talked of various subjects before I took my leave of this fine gentleman."

* * *

"I must add a sad postscript to the above, in the year 1823. I have just received intelligence that Mr. Gordon had died in his home. He was a pillar of the Worshipful Company of Distillers, to which he was admitted in 1792 and of which he was Renter Warden in 1808 and Upper Warden in 1810. A loss to our great City."

_1830_ YOUTH AT THE HELM

The coppersmith was astonished by the youthfulness of his customer. However, the man came from a respected family and had impeccable financial references, though the smith understood he was not yet of age.

"I require," said Charles Tanqueray, "your most modern stills, both large and small, for the making of cordial spirits and for compounding rectified spirit with ingredients to produce gin. I am concerned to make in my Bloomsbury Distillery nothing but the choicest liquors. You have the estimated costs I requested?"

"Yes, sir, and be assured we employ the latest techniques, the best materials, and take no short-cuts in manufacture."

"I am confident you do, or I would not now be talking with you."

The still-maker consulted a paper. "The smithing of a two hundred gallon still will stand you in at £275, with a charge of 15 shillings per gallon for any size in excess. You will be aware, sir, that I refer to total capacity in gallons, not the working quantity that is considerably less. The copper itself is extra at 14 pence the pound."

"Yes, I am entirely familiar with such details. Pray continue."

"I expect you may wish for stills of large capacity, such as are employed by the great gin houses in Clerkenwell."

"I need at least one such apparatus."

"I can, sir, do you a 500-gallon pot-still of the newest type, weighing half a ton, for an all-in price of £382 and 10 shillings."

"I like your precision."

"It is a point of pride with me, sir."

"I think we shall do business. If we conclude an arrangement, I wish to be in production within six months."

"That may be done, sire, so far as I am concerned."

"I have arranged installation; I have engaged experts. Now here is what I want from you . . ."

* * *

The coppersmith may indeed have been surprised at Charles Tanqueray's youth – he was twenty – yet that was a time when careers started much earlier than today. Educated at the famous London school, St. Paul's, Charles showed no interest in idling at university: his tastes were for the practical and experimental with a leaning towards chemistry in its social applications. Generations previously, his forebears had been goldsmiths in Metz, an occupation sustained by later members of the family when, along with many Huguenots, they became refugees from France to the enrichment of several countries, none more so than England. The first English Tanqueray, David, was a gold and silversmith, operating in a fashionable part of the City of Westminster. He was naturalised by Act of Parliament in 1708. He was famous in his craft and was appointed a supplier to King George II. He died in 1726. The Tanquerays then showed an inclination towards the Church, producing several notable clerics.

The decision by Charles Tanqueray to enter commerce caused no raised eyebrows: he was expected to lead an industrious life. No Tanqueray was inclined to be described as a man of leisure, even if being an early 19th century Church of England rural rector could amount to much the same thing. Charles was the son of a clergyman. Earlier, his choice of profession might have been criticised, but it was by now something with which a gentleman could be associated. Alexander Gordon, with whom the Tanquerays were connected distantly by marriage, had recently died as an honoured citizen of London. The greatest gin distiller of the day, Sheriff Booth, had in the previous year gained acclaim for public spiritedness in financing Captain Ross's second expedition to find the legendary North-West Passage. Felix Booth had been a friend of the Duke of Clarence, and

33

thus of the newly ascended King William IV. Gin distilling had moved a long way: it was an ornament of London's industry. Charles was entering the trade at just the right moment and he was determined that his Bloomsbury Distillery, sited so as to use pure water from adjacent Finsbury spa, should above all become renowned for quality.

Soon, Charles Tanqueray's stoneware crocks – he did not deal in bulk casked gin for ordinary taverns – were to be seen in the better class of grocers and wine and spirit merchants, and in discerning households. We must not think of gin at that time as being a single product in today's sense. One could choose from a wide selection of fruit-flavoured gins, or traditional Dutch styles or Old Tom, which all distillers made. There was unsweetened gin, which you could flavour as you liked: of that we shall hear more in the next chapter.

The entry of ambitious, competent and, from his background, conscientious Charles Tanqueray into the distilling business was to have remarkable consequences for London as the world's gin capital.

1834   SPIRITUOUS PALACES

By the time he was twenty-one Charles Dickens had escaped from dire poverty, from the wheedling fiscal prevarications of the father he was later to immortalise. As a young contributor to *The Monthly* magazine, he

saw his future as a journalist, a chronicler of his times. Already he was demonstrating the perceptive eye, the flair for character and detail, the knack of capturing atmosphere in words, that would be displayed with precocious maturity in but a few years time when Mr. Pickwick would be joyously received. His observations, under the pseudonym Boz, were attracting favourable notice, for he brought to the affluent vivid verbal portraits of people and places which, existing only around the corner, were often as foreign to his readers as an African jungle.

Four years earlier, the duty on beer had been abolished, in another attempt to wean the metropolitan masses from addiction to strong liquor, and anyone might now sell beer after obtaining an easy and inexpensive license. As with most legislation about drink, the Act had unforeseen results. Dickens was aware that it had led to intense competition for drinkers' custom. Those licensees, and brewers, who could raise the funds, built magnificent new public houses or embellished older ones. He was in two minds on the subject. Thus Boz the reformer wrote: "Gin-drinking is a great vice in England . . . Until you improve the homes of the poor, or persuade a half-famished wretch not to seek relief in temporary oblivion of his own misery . . . gin shops will increase in number and splendour. If Temperance societies would suggest an antidote against hunger, filth and foul air . . . gin-palaces would be numbered amongst things that were [of the past]."

Yet Dickens the realist rather approved the splendiferous edifices that replaced many a sordid drinking-den:

"All is light and brilliancy. The hum of many voices issued from that splendid gin-shop . . . the gay building with fantastically ornamented parapet, the illuminated clock, the plate-glass windows surrounded by stucco rosettes, and its profusion of gas-lights in richly-gilt burners, is perfectly dazzling when contrasted with the darkness and dirt [outside in the street]. The interior is even gayer than the exterior. A bar of French-polished mahogany, elegantly carved, extends the whole width of the place; and there are two side-aisles of great casks, painted green and gold . . . bearing such inscriptions as 'Old Tom, 549', 'Young Tom, 360', 'Samson, 1421' – figures agreeing, we assume, with 'gallons' . . . Behind the counter are two showily-dressed damsels with large necklaces, dispensing spirits and 'compounds' . . . The two old washerwomen, who are seated on the little bench to the left of the bar, are rather overcome by the young ladies who officiate. They receive their quartern of gin and peppermint with considerable deference."

Charles Dickens must have been familiar with Thomas Rowlandson's amusingly scathing cartoons of gin-shops two decades previously. He was to find his own brilliant illustrator in George Cruickshank who, with all the fury of a reformed dipsomaniac, was to depict real and fancied horrors of "demon gin", to the delight of the Temperance movement, yet in many a caricature unconsciously advertising the attractions of what he attacked.

* * *

The London which Dickens often described set the tone for the rest of England. Gin Palaces, often rivalling the glories of those in the capital, sprang up in the burgeoning industrial cities. A massive migration from the countryside continued with the increasing demand for mill and factory workers. Families, by inclination or necessity, left tumbledown cottages, whose picturesque qualities were more apparent to urban visitors than to their inhabitants; they abandoned turved hovels and savoured the delights of little terraced houses, row on row, of which at least the roofs did not leak much. However, though these "model dwellings" – for the more fortunate migrants – did not suffer from rustic discomforts, also missing were bucolic pastimes and pleasures. A tiny backyard was not a vegetable plot nor a cobbled street a village green. Yet these new industrial hands had more ready money than before, and down the road was a gleaming Gin Palace offering glamorous surroundings, social exchange, and drink. The Gin Palace was for thousands their sole centre for recreation – man, woman, and child.

Though the Truck Act of 1831 had outlawed payment of any part of wages in kind, some employers, with the connivance of landlords, would

arrange to hand out wages in a Gin Palace – and how many men took home their money intact?

Despite the intentions of Parliament, gin was prominent in everyday life: its extraordinary popularity was witnessed by the virulence with which it was attacked. As he became well-to-do, Dickens relished the good things of life and enjoyed the conviviality of a fine tavern. His great grandson, Cedric Dickens, has reminded us that the author was partial to a glass of gin punch and liked the ritual of preparing such mixes. Gin, or Geneva, was often mentioned in his books, by no means with the opprobrium shown by Boz.

Dickens lived into the period that witnessed gin's re-birth in a modern role. His well-stocked cellar at Gad's Hill indicated a catholic taste. When catalogued for sale after his death in 1870, it held many cases of fine wines, dozens of Scotch whiskey (sic), varieties of cognac and liqueurs – and 16 bottles of Old Geneva plus 36 bottles of "London cordial gin", distiller not stated but bought from a celebrated firm of London merchants.

* * *

"Du gin, du gin – à plein verre, garçon!
Dans ses flots d'or, cette rude boisson
Roule le ciel et l'oublie de soi-même."

Auguste Barbier
(French poet, 19th. century)

NOTES

1822 RISE OF A GREAT COMPANY

The known facts have been used to construct a short picture of the early days of what was to become the world's premier gin business. In the year in question, Gordon's were prominent, but not leader, in the London gin trade. There were some half-dozen big distillers and a host of minor ones. Felix Booth was the largest producer, and Boord's, possibly founded as early as 1726, was important. Amongst forgotten distilleries was that of Israel Wilkes, who benefited from

being the father of John Wilkes (1727–97), the populist and unruly politician. (John's cousin, Elizabeth Wilkes, married a Booth and from that union stemmed the remarkable American Booth family of actors, whose escutcheon was sadly marred by John Wilkes Booth, President Lincoln's assassin).

* * *

The reference to the Rev. John Skinner is to highlight the spread of gin-drinking to the countryside. John Skinner (b. 1772) for a long time held the living of Camerton, near

Bath, a small community of coal-miners and farmers. He had great problems with both his patrons and his flock, a drunken lot of whose gin-drinking he constantly complained. His sad, if compelling, "Journal Of a Somerset Rector, 1803–34" (Oxford University Press) depicts the reverse side to the idyllic rural English life beloved by romantics. Skinner shot himself dead in 1839.

* * *

Clerkenwell, the district in which Alexander Gordon finally established his company, played an essential role in London's triumph as *the* gin distilling city. (Clerkenwell became part of the Borough of Finsbury which was absorbed into an enlarged Islington under Edward Heath's disastrous reorganisation of London). Because of its copious good water, Clerkenwell was much favoured by distillers, brewers and millers. For less obvious reasons, it became a clock-making centre. Mr. Whitbread's supplies came from the Choice Well: hence Chiswell Street, where there is no longer a brewery but which houses the firm's headquarters to this day. Turnmill Street has been mentioned: it recalls a lost stream of sufficient power to turn three water-mills. This was the Holeburn (brook in the hollow) which joined the Fleet river – a festering open sewer – in the area now called Holborn (Ho'bun). Cow Cross Street is where there was once a fording place across the Hole-burn for cattle on their way to Smithfield Market – close to Mr. Gordon's home.

The Clerks' Well (Clerkenwell) appears to have been not much used in historic times and was so little considered that it was built over and lost for many years, being rediscovered in 1924, though it is marked on the earliest extant map of London (c. 1560). It was referred to in a manuscript of 1174 and is thought to be of immense antiquity. Traditionally, parish clerks used to assemble beside it to enact religious dramas, possibly an adaptation of rites from pre-Christian Britain.

I understand the Clerks' Well may still be visited by appointment, though I do not recommend it as a tourist attraction. It is unimpressive, only six feet deep, more a spring than a well: it maintains an absolutely constant level. On my sole visit, twenty years ago, the custodian, who opened the dingy cellar for my inspection, took a filthy old broom from a dusty corner and agitated the surface of the water so that my photograph – which did not develop – might be livelier. "It is perfectly good to drink," he said, handing me a rusting mug, "It's traditional to take some." I am all for tradition, but on this occasion – as journalists traditionally write – I made my excuses and left.

* * *

Export of London gin, the fiscal handicap of which Alexander Gordon is shown as deploring, was eventually freed through the intervention of his rival, Sir Felix Booth. He instigated at considerable expense, through his export agents, a Private Bill in Parliament which lifted excise duties from gin sent abroad. The measure was passed in 1850, the year of Sir Felix's death. It proved of much benefit to all leading gin companies and enhanced the status of London gin.

1830 YOUTH AT THE HELM

The figures quoted for making stills are from a contemporary document in the possession of John Tanqueray, of the present Charles Tanqueray & Co., a direct descendant of Charles.

* * *

The Ross expedition did not return home until 1833. Failing in his main purpose, Ross plotted the location of the North Magnetic Pole and made useful discoveries. In honour of his patron, a large penninsula in Arctic Canada is named Boothia. (There is also a topographical Tanqueray association with the Dominion's frozen North.) Sir Felix received his baronetcy from his friend, the

King. He had put up £20,000 of his own money after the government reneged on various promises.

* * *

The Tanqueray stoneware jars were the feature of the trade until 1900.

* * *

A price list of 1895 from W. A. Taylor & Co. of New York illustrates a bottle of Tanqueray's "Finest Old Tom", with the caption, "The Bloomsbury Distillery, established 1757". This implies that Charles took over, rather than founded, the concern. There is no evidence for that, so the claim must be attributed to clerical error – or the importer's historical enthusiasm.

1834 SPIRITUOUS PALACES

"Gin Palace" started pejoratively; then, like "Mother's Ruin", it became affectionately jocular as a description. The Gin Palace, which of course sold much else besides gin, flourished way beyond the Victorian period that was its heyday. Despite brewery vandalism, a few prime examples survive as architectural monuments. There have even been attempts to construct replicas, though solid mahogany is too expensive and the art of making cut-glass mirrors in quantity seems to have been lost.

"Mother's Ruin" is archaic, yet still part of the language, which was once rich in synonyms for gin. There is an enormous list of historical descriptions for "Parliamentary Brandy", some of which continued in use after the need to evade 18th century "Gin Acts" had disappeared. Typical are – Cuckold's Comfort, Last Shift, The Gripe, King Theodore of Tuscany, Tom Roe, The Baulk, Ladies' Delight, Daffy . . . the reasons behind some names are lost. Blue Lightning, Cat Water, Cold Cream, Royal Poverty, Frog's Cream, Misery . . . There

were many more. There was Cockney rhyming slang – Brian (O'Lynn), and in Dickens's day he might have encountered the terms for gin peculiar to people in certain professions: Eye-Water (printers), Lap (chorus girls) or Duke (upper servants).

Old Tom, starting as a general description, became associated with a special style of gin. Tradition says that word got around that a cat had fallen into a vat at a certain distillery, giving the gin a particular flavour! The most probable true derivation of Old Tom, as generally accepted by its many former devotees, is from Thomas Chamberlain, an early experimenter in compounding gin: at one time he was commemorated on labels for Boord's Old Tom gin which was a particularly popular brand. It is still occasionally made for the Finnish market. Old Tom is relished in Lapland: the Finnish alcohol monopoly also makes it.

BACKGROUND

RESUMÉ OF ASPECTS OF GIN IN FIRST THREE-QUARTERS OF 19TH CENTURY

1800–1815 – The Napoleonic wars, by concentrating national attention on vital matters of survival, brought to Britain a degree of comparative sobriety – comparative, that is, with the extreme excesses of the previous century. However, there was laxity in enforcement of regulations, much evasion of excise taxes and a growth in illegal outlets for gin. Socially, there was a growing revulsion against the drunkenness lately common to all classes, though the depth of this feeling should not be exaggerated. A notion that temperance was not unmanly was reinforced by the spread of coffee-drinking from an upper-class mode to a universal fashion. Tax concessions made coffee a cheap beverage. Water supplies were very bad: water was only to be drunk in most places at recognised risk to health. Not that the popularity of gin suffered greatly, and it was soon to enjoy renewed strength of hold on the mass population. It might also be added that, for people on a very poor diet, the heavy, sweet gins provided calories in stimulating form.

1815 – A sidelight on the Battle of Waterloo: When Marshal Blücher was marching his Prussians in vital support of Wellington, he was thrown by his

horse, which caused such dismay in his army that their further progress to the battlefield was in doubt. The Marshal was revived with a mixture of gin and onions and was able to bring his reinforcement to the British, without which Napoleon might not have been defeated. It is not clear whether the gin-onion remedy was applied externally or as a potion: that does not alter its historic importance.

1830–1835 – See *1834* above.

1860 – Gladstone, as Chancellor of the Exchequer and a proponent of free trade, greatly reduced the taxes on wine imports. Inexpensive wine flowed into Britain – to the detriment of beer sales rather than those of gin.

1861 – Grocers were given leave to retail wines and spirits. It was intended that this liberalisation should promote cheap wine as a substitute for spirits. In the event, it simply increased easy access to gin.

1871 – Under Gladstone's premiership, a Bill was proposed that would effectively halve the numbers of licensed premises in England and Wales. Opposition was furious. In the House of Lords, then a body holding firm views on the freedom of the individual against state encroachment, even episcopal wrath was engendered: denouncing the Gladstonian proposal, a bishop thundered that, "I would rather see England free than England sober." (No wonder "English Bishop" was a popular strong punch!)*.

1872 – Gladstone put before the House of Commons a much altered Bill, but still too restrictive for the majority of electors.

1874 – An enraged public threw Gladstone's Liberals out at the general election. The ex-Prime Minister wrote that he had "been borne down in a torrent of gin" – a fate that would surely have been welcomed by a high proportion of the populace.

We now approach a new era for gin, aided by a fresh development in the product itself.

---

* After I had used this quotation in a letter in the *Daily Telegraph* (16.8.88), that newspaper published a response from Mr. Victor Hatley, of Northampton, giving a fuller version of what the Bishop (William Magee of Peterborough) said when the Gladstone Bill was debated in the House of Lords (2.5.1872):

"It would be better that England should be free than that England should be compulsorily sober." Bishop Magee, a strong Temperance supporter, added, "I would distinctly prefer freedom to sobriety, because with freedom we might in the end attain sobriety; but in the other alternative we should eventually lose both freedom and sobriety."

These are words of which all promoters of Prohibition should be reminded.

4

*A V*OGUE FOR *D*RYNESS

1874 MRS. CRUMBLE'S TEA PARTY

Picture a comfortable, over-furnished drawing-room in a pleasant, though not particularly large, late Georgian terrace house. It is situated in an up-and-coming London district, off Gray's Inn Road. Its owner, Mr. Timothy Crumble, is at his haberdashery business in the nearby City. Mrs. Crumble, who has some pretensions to gentility (for her father was a magistrate in her native provincial town), is At Home to a select group of local ladies, wives of substantial tradesmen for the most part. With ripe social hyperbole, she refers to this as her "salon".

Tea has been served by the sole male servitor, Herbert, known by Mrs. Crumble as "our butler." He has removed the elaborate silver service. The new, much admired, gas chandelier has been lit. Mrs. Crumble then issues the welcome words, hallowed by repetition: "And now, ladies, I think we may take a little white wine" (pronounced "waite wane"). The ladies are familiar with the euphemism. As if by pre-arrangement – which it is – Herbert reappears, bearing a large salver on which repose eight glasses and an ornate decanter: this carries a neck label inscribed Nig. Separately, there is a bottle of water ("spa water" Mrs. Crumble emphasises) for individual dilution.

"Today I have a little surprise for you," announces Mrs. Crumble. Her guests titter with anticipation. Their hostess is renowned in her restricted circle for her sense of modish novelty. Was she not the first of their acquaintance to hide the immodest nudity of the bulbous legs of her pianoforte with frilly integuments? Had she not some years previously pioneered – soon to be copied by her friends – the use of lace antimacassars to protect sofas from the fragrant but extremely oleaginous dressing with which gentlemen were treating their hair? As Herbert pours limpid fluid into glasses and profers them on a silver tray, Mrs. Crumble continues: "Contrary to appearances, this is not our usual refreshment. It is a new style of – to employ the common term – of gin. My supplier, who is purveyor of groceries to Her Majesty" – she gives a sort of loyal nod – "calls this his Special Unsweetened. He buys only from the best distillers and says that this type of spirit has, in crude form, long existed for the lower orders, who add cordials to it. Only lately has it been refined sufficiently to obtain the favour of the gentry. It is, I understand, recommended by physicians who follow the dietary system evolved by Mr. Banting."

One of the ladies opines that she has lately read Mr. Banting's tract. "Indeed," says Mrs. Crumble. "*I* read it when it was published years ago. I recall that Mr. Banting is against sugar and sweetened beverages." She takes a substantial sip from her glass and wipes her lips on a minute cambric handkerchief. The assembly do the same. One lady, for something to say, suggests that the spirit has "a pleasingly delicate smell".

"Yes, the boo*kay* is delectable," agrees Mrs. Crumble with corrective emphasis. Mellowing, the ladies drink and gossip. Complimentary noises are made, even by those who would have preferred the traditional heavier Hollands. Mrs. Crumble depresses the ornate new brass bell-pull.

"A fresh decanter of the same, please, Herbert."

1875   FOLLOW THAT TREND

"It is remarkable, sir, how greatly the demand for our unsweetened gin has increased of late."

Charles Waugh Tanqueray regarded his chief clerk: he encouraged his senior employees to discuss matters with him unasked. Even at twenty-seven, Charles was an imposing presence. He had a striking resemblance to the Prince of Wales, a source of pride to him and, as it became more pronounced in later life, was to be an occasional embarrassment to strangers who momentarily mistook him for Edward VII: that lay far ahead.

The first Charles Tanqueray had died in 1868, so Charles Waugh found himself head of the family at twenty, which was precisely the age when his father had started business in the Bloomsbury Distillery as recounted in the previous chapter. Charles Waugh Tanqueray was ready for the task. He had thrived on the rigours of Rugby School where the traditions prevailed that had been established by Thomas Arnold, legendary founder of that most private of institutions, the British public school, with its creed of "strength through misery." Arnold's educational system aimed at producing upright Christian gentlemen of forceful character yet with social conscience: he would have been proud of Charles Waugh Tanqueray.

"I had taken notice of this phenomenon, Arkwright," he said. "Only a few days ago I was approached to supply a few jars of unsweetened to Brooks's Club in St. James's, whereas they have always taken Choicest Old Tom. The steward informed me that younger members have taken to drinking gin twists and gin with vermouth wine and even stranger oddities which the Americans call cocktails."

"An extraordinary name, sir. I confess I have not encountered it before."

"Maybe we shall hear little more of it. You know the Americans, always going for something novel. There was that Yankee barkeeper, who wrote a strange book a few years ago – all about mixing drinks. It created quite a stir in some quarters. Perhaps that's where the clubmen get their notions – though I doubt many of 'em read books beyond *Ruff's Guide to the Turf.* Anyway, it seems unsweetened is better for their mixtures than cordial ones or Holland's."

"But, with respect, sir, that alone cannot account for our extra sales of unsweetened. The City bars are taking more, and so are some of our clients amongst the better grocers and wine merchants. Also, Mr. Jobson of your export department tells me there is an accretion of overseas demand, particularly from our American agents."

"Unsweetened gin is scarcely new, Mr. Arkwright. You know we have always made it. My father had a recipe for his "Twenty-Two Percent" which contained no sugar at all. Mind you, I do not know how much of it was then made. It may turn out a good thing that we have it in our list. How are other distilleries doing with unsweetened? You have a reputation for keeping your ear to the ground: I mostly only hear what my friends wish me to."

"Thank you, sir. I have information that rather more unsweetened than usual is coming out of Goswell Street, and that the Red Lion Distillery may be about to launch a new style, somewhat lighter than usual, though I have no idea what it is to be called. I think Boord will continue to specialise in Old Tom. I don't feel the Bishops, of Finsbury, will be much interested in any change of fashion: they are essentially cordial people. I cannot speak for any others. Personally I have no contact with Millbank, Chelsea or Fulham. Perhaps, sir, you could ascertain from fellow-members of the Rectifiers' Club whether this additional call for unsweetened is more than a fad."

"I doubt my friends in the Rectifiers will tell me much: they are rivals, too, you must appreciate. I have a presentiment that what we are speaking of is more than a passing whim of fashion. We do a superior sort of trade. So if our unsweetened is gaining increasing demand, that means that it is not going to the lower taverns – probably for blending into their own meretricious wares – but is being purchased for, or by, the wealthier class of person."

"That would indicate a revolutionary trend, sir."

"One must be prepared to follow trends, be prepared for them, or one may be left behind. But here we come up against a factor which could impede a wider demand for unsweetened. In terms of modern commerce it lacks a name. I mean, people demand Hollands or sloe gin or suchlike and know what they are getting. The term "unsweetened" has a descriptive connotation but it has no particular appeal. I find it difficult to explain my feeling: it lacks something. It is a negative – *un*sweetened – yes, that is the trouble."

Mr. Tanqueray paused. Then his chief clerk said, "May I make a suggestion? Something has just occurred to me."

"Go ahead, Arkwright. I value any ideas."

"Well, sir, I have this young nephew who is in the wine trade with a most respectable house. They have a comfortable clientele and sell a large amount of champagne. Of this, the French are now making quite a lot to what they call the "English taste" – wine which is much less sweet than the wine to which we have been accustomed. In the trade this is called dry champagne to distinguish it from the usual style. My nephew tells me that word has got around that the house of Ayala's '65, which they call extra dry, has become a favourite with His Royal Highness the Prince of Wales . . ." instinctively Charles Tanqueray glanced briefly at the large mirror on his office wall ". . . and, as a result, dry champagne has become quite the rage with fashionable folk, even if they do not all like it. So I have just thought, sir . . ."

"A very good thought. I have drunk such champagne – and found it tart to my palate – though perhaps one would acquire a taste for it. Dry. Dry. A succinct and excellent word. Have some trial labels run off, Arkwright. I much commend your notion. Tanqueray's Unsweetened Dry . . . No, clumsy. Tanqueray's Dry gin. No, not quite right. Let's see – what about Tanqueray's *London* Dry gin? No possible confusion there."

* * *

"The friends of the grape may boast of rich Cape,
Hock, Claret, Madeira and Lachryma Christ,
But this muzzle of mine was never so fine
As to value them more than a jug of gin-twist."

William Maginn (1793–1842)
from "A Thirst-imony in Favour of Gin-twist."

NOTES

1874 MRS. CRUMBLE'S TEA PARTY

"White wine" was quite a usual euphemism for gin in feminine circles at this time. Gin was being drunk at all levels of society but it was not entirely respectable. "Nig" was an extreme example of Victorian prudery and is thought to have been used so that the word itself should not be seen in a respectable household. However, a counter-theory is that, rather improbably, it was a device to deceive servants – presumably also deficient in sense of taste. Or was "nig" simply Cockney back-slang? It would have been carrying a joke a bit far to make silver labels for Nig: though they are rare, they were produced.

* * *

It is entirely reasonable to suppose that William Banting had a direct influence in popularising unsweetened gin. His "Letter on Corpulence" was published in 1863, when he was 66 years old. It engendered great interest: 50,000 copies were quickly sold and it gradually permeated into the national consciousness. The Banting diet, evolved with a medical friend, was both simple and sensible. It included plenty of meat (including bacon but not fresh pork), cut down on starches and avoided sugar. Thus claret, sherry and Madeira (presumably in their drier forms) were in order; port and champagne (then normally a sweet wine) were out. After a year on this far from Spartan regime, Mr. Banting lost 46 lbs and

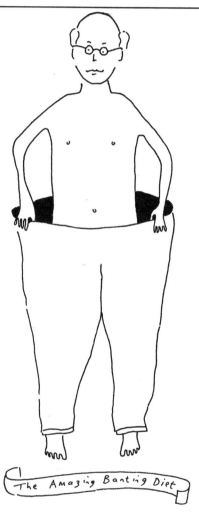

The Amazing Banting Diet

had reduced his waist measurement by 12½ inches. He lived merrily to the age of eighty-one. His tract long continued in print – and might with minor amendations apply today. In my youth, when one of my elders was trying to reduce weight, they were still said to be "banting."

1875 FOLLOW THAT TREND

There is, of course, absolutely no evidence that Mr. Tanqueray coined the description London Dry Gin. We do not know who did. Probably it was adopted concurrently by several distillers: the exclusive Rectifiers' Club may have chosen the words. Early advertisements usually carried additional emphasis such as "positively contains no sugar", indicating that "dry" was not yet fully understood by the general public. The princely influence on "dryness" is factual.

The first London Dry gins were not quite like today's: they were more aromatic, as contemporary formulae demonstrate. By the turn of the century, however, dry was the type most widely drunk, though Old Tom retained a strong following for at least another generation and there was a considerable demand for Hollands (which had reverted to meaning Geneva imported from the Netherlands).

That "dry" took some time to be accepted is indicated by the 1895 list referred to in chapter 4 (Notes). It quotes no "dry", but Tanqueray's "unsweetened" at the same price as Old Tom – $8.75 per 12-bottle case (or £1.80 at the exchange rate then prevailing!).

* * *

Around the period with which we are dealing, the first American unsweetened (dry) gin was made in Ohio by the Fleischmann brothers who established their distillery in 1870. But in the famous (to connoisseurs of drinking history) book by Harry Johnson – of which more anon – Old Tom or Holland are

specified wherever a type is quoted: sometimes he simply says "gin." Incidentally, this publication, written for bartenders, exemplifies a more spacious attitude than ours: the instructions for mixing some drinks start: "Hand the bottle of gin to the customer."!

* * *

As London Dry gradually spread throughout the world for a description of the principal style of gin – becoming drier, less aromatic, over the years – it lost its exclusively topographical association. There are countries where inclusion of London on a label is allowable only if the gin is imported from Britain, but for the most part the term is generic. However, it is London (or English) distillers whose gins command the widest respect and sales, and those made in England carry extra prestige. Worldwide, English dry gin (with or without the London tag) dominates the quality market, whether imported or made locally by English distillers' subsidiaries or licencees. Globally, the biggest-selling fine gin is Gordon's: of English gins Gilbey's is number two. In the U.S.A. Gordon's shares the top of the domestic market with Seagram's, the Canadian company founded by an Englishman. Tanqueray went to the head of the imported gin chart in 1985.

In later sections of this book, when gin (without qualification) is mentioned, it means (London) dry gin.

Caveat emptor: In certain countries there is considerable counterfeiting of famous gin brands, also the production of indifferent gins in bottles whose labels are designed to look much like well-known ones. In bars, re-refilling of imported gin bottles with very ordinary cheap local "gin" is a common practice in tourist hotels. Let the holidaymaker be cautious – and read those labels carefully in shops of strange places

* * *

I trust that Scots and Irish people will not be annoyed by my constant reference to England. It is England, and particularly its capital, that are central to gin's story. For obvious reasons, historically Scotland has been little concerned with gin: today, of course, it is as widely distributed there as anywhere else. In historical terms, the same applies to Ireland: comparatively recently, gin production was started there.

* * *

I have jumped ahead, yet I feel these ancillary matters deserve attention here as relating to the rise of Dry gin. It was the enormous eventual success of this new style that marked a turning point in the product's long journey. Dry gin pushed gin into areas formerly devoted to other spirits: it gave a fresh meaning to gin for people who had not cared for earlier types. Introduction of Dry gin gave gin a "class" it had previously lacked. Gin was ready to move into modern times and eminently placed to adapt to a changing world.

* * *

"A *small* gin is no more than a dirty glass."

Jay Dee.

Charles Tanqueray, 1810–68

5

I_NTO_ M_ODERN_ T_IMES_

Gin came of age in the 1890s. Various factors helped it. The introduction of dry gin was of prime importance. But there were other events that benefited gin. The effects of the phylloxera plague that ravaged the world's vineyards were seen in a dearth of cheap grape brandy: many brandy-drinkers turned to Scotch whisky, and others tried gin, and liked it. Much gin was being exported, largely to the Empire, then in its full flowering: returning imperial servants of the Crown did much to give gin social acceptability, as did its naval association. We shall illustrate that later. Americans of wealth were travelling to Europe in the great liners. They brought drinking patterns with them that Europeans, and particularly the English, found amusing – cocktails: rather daring, if not quite right in good society.

So the gin trade was doing nicely. At one end, the Gin Palaces were thriving: at the other, gin was growing ever more popular with the well-to-do: the aristocracy did not disdain having it on their sideboards. While some distilleries in London, such as Wilkes's, had disappeared or been absorbed, new names had appeared on the scene: competition was increasingly fierce. The time was ripe for rationalisation. One such arrangement was eventually to make an impact on the gin commerce that its progenitors could scarcely have dreamed of.

1898 A CRUCIAL DEAL

Charles Waugh Tanqueray, whom we have met as a young man, had pushed his Bloomsbury Distillery into prominence at the top end of the gin trade. His agents were active overseas. As sole proprietor of his business, his financial position was strong. Charles Waugh Tanqueray was now known to all and sundry as "Boss", a word, in its modern connotation, recently imported from the U.S.A. He enjoyed this soubriquet. Now he was talking to Reginald Currie, head of Gordon & Company for the past six years.

We had better explain the situation: why Currie? The names of several distilleries famous in their day have passed into oblivion. One such is John Currie's, perhaps once the most important in England outside London. They were established in the 18th century in the salubrious suburb of Bromley, Kent, and became major suppliers of fine neutral spirit to Gordon & Company. A decade before the moment with which we are dealing, Charles Gordon, grandson of the founder, had retired, severing the last family link with the company. Currie's acquired the business, customarily referred to as The House, and after four years, Reginald Currie assumed personal control. That is why he was closeted with Charles Tanqueray in the latter's office.

"The point is, Mr. Currie, that the gin trade is spread amongst too great a number of companies – fragmented is the description now favoured by financiers. Apart from ourselves, we have Booth's, and the Nicholsons and the Curtis's; and the Gilbey family, the fine vintners, have come in; and there's Burrough's in Chelsea, and Robert Burnett in Fulham; Coates in Plymouth; Greenall in the North-West, and the new firm just formed to take on the interests of the late Mr. Seager – and those are just a few names that come to mind. There are numerous minor distillers, in London and the provinces, all trying for their bit of the business."

"I agree, Mr. Tanqueray. Yet, with gin being ever more demanded across the whole population, newcomers must inevitably be attracted to enter the trade. I know of several brewers who are anxious to make their own gin."

"That is to be resisted so far as it can be. But we cannot resist the tide of progress, nor would I wish to. We live in an age of commercial growth, where there is little future in the small or timid. Power lies with the big and strong. One needs the strength to beat competition, strength to maintain high production without sacrifice of quality, strength to finance expansion and to employ modern methods of advertising. Ours is an old trade and in many ways it is old-fashioned. This is a time of unlimited opportunity – for the strong and enterprising."

"In unity is strength? Do I correctly guess the way your mind is working, Mr. Tanqueray?"

"I think you do, Mr. Currie. Before you say anything more, please let me continue. Look at it this way. You have sales beyond mine in the mass market; your company's name is well established with a large section of the general public. We are both doing well abroad, which is profitable, where there are vast untapped outlets. On the other hand, you must have extended yourselves to the limit to purchase The House . . ."

"You are not suggesting you buy us out!" exclaimed Reginald Currie. "That is out of the question. We did not buy for a re-sale."

"No, I am not. Please hear me out. I have, on my side, a high class of trade, complementing yours, and I have ample liquidity of funds." Charles Tanqueray placed emphasis on those last words. "What I am recommending is a joining of our forces, to exploit our several strengths in unison instead of in competition."

"An amalgamation. I was half-hoping you were thinking that way. It could have great possibilities."

"Not great – immense beyond any present ambitions we might individually entertain. I believed you would like the idea. Here I have, Mr. Currie" – Charles Tanqueray took a file of documents from a drawer in his desk – "draft proposals outlining the scheme for a joint company."

"I can see why they call you Boss, Mr. Tanqueray."

"You may so call me if you like, Mr. Currie."

"I fancy we would be joint 'bosses' should this project come to fruition." Reginald Currie glanced at the top paper of the sheaf he held. "I see you tentatively call the combination Tanqueray-Gordon."

"You have objections?" said Charles Tanqueray rather briskly.

"We are senior in age, and alphabetically G precedes T."

"On the other hand, I would be investing rather more cash than you in the venture. There are no Gordons left in the company, as there would be a Tanqueray. I am sure Charles Gordon, if asked, would not mind: he is far happier with his inventions than he ever was in business. Our main product would, I suggest, be continued to be called Gordon's dry gin. In fact, I know it should be. Tanqueray would go on as before. In combination, we shall take advantage of every opportunity for expansion."

"Very well, then. You seem confident we shall join up."

"I am."

"I do approve in principle."

"Then, Mr. Currie, let us personally shake on it, and may not our lawyers' pettyfogging details long delay the consummation of our deal."

"Here is my hand, Mr. Tanqueray. Let us hope we are enabled to set a fresh standard in the trade of which we are both proud."

* * *

"This calls the Church to deprecate our sin,
And hurls the thunder of the laws on Gin."
Alexander Pope

51

1910 BEFORE THE DELUGE

The first decade of the 20th century reached its apogee with the closing of the Edwardian era. It found gin in a very different social position to that pertaining in late Victorian times. Earlier chapters of illustrative episodes traced gin's gradual emergence from the shadows: there was no ephocal point at which the spirit, once reviled as the opiate of the masses, became acceptable to the whole general public. This is a good moment to recapitulate. I deem the most important factors, to the time of the Great War, to have been – the evolution of London Dry gin as a subtly distinctive product; the reorganisation of English distilling and vast improvement in the quality of the product: the discovery of gin's virtues by respectable women; and the influence of Empire. Amongst contributors to this triumph were the temporary dearth of brandy through the phylloxera plague (though Scotch whisky benefited much more) and the adoption of the American habit of drinking cocktails by a small, fashion-setting segment of English Society (but American impact was to be much stronger later).

So 1910 may be said to be mid-term in our story. It saw the opening of Britain's first true Cocktail Bar, the Criterion in London's Piccadilly Circus: it was not that much different to other smart bars – it was the title that was significant. London Dry gin now enjoyed international prestige: it was a considerable export business. In Britain, gin had moved from the pub and was on its way to the palace; it was being enjoyed by patricians as well as by the proletariat; it had lost its feminine connotation along with its disreputable one. The lights might be about to go out over Europe: when they were rekindled, gin's flame was destined to burn the more brightly.

1915 A WAR BONUS

Gin benefited from World War I in a peculiar way. With the failure to "beat the Germans by Christmas" (1914), things were going far from well for the Anglo-French forces bogged down in Flanders. There was a shortage of artillery shells amounting to a major scandal. The Prime Minister, Herbert Asquith, was under pressure: he was shortly to be succeeded by David Lloyd George as head of a coalition government. Under trying circumstances, it is normal for politicians to look for a scapegoat. In this instance, an individual was not available, or was too powerful, for censure – so a product was substituted.

Someone came up with the notion that workers, prosperous in comparison to their pre-war condition, were producing insufficient munitions not through managerial shortcomings or shortage of raw materials but because they were spending too much on strong liquor, which was making for inefficiency and undue absenteeism. The faults lay elsewhere, but this was an easily acceptable theory. Had not the King himself banned alcohol from his household for the duration? Some administrative genius noted that consumption of straight grain whisky had increased with the rise in industrial wages. Grain whisky, now almost unknown in retail commerce though in its matured form vital to production of blended Scotch, was then a very popular and cheap spirit: it was not matured or minimally so. So the Cabinet was persuaded to bring in regulations, under an amendment to the Defence of the Realm Act, making it obligatory for all whisky (and analogous spirits such as brandy) to be matured in cask for at least three years before sale.

The new regulation instantly cut off supplies of inexpensive grain whisky: the Scotch whisky industry complained that it faced ruin – though in the long term it was destined greatly to gain by a general improvement in quality and prestige through the compulsory maturing that had hitherto been confined to superior blends or fine straight malts. An immediate result was a boost for gin. Gin, a rectified spirit requiring no maturing, was unaffected by the new law: except for inevitable wartime shortages, it prospered. Traditional drinkers of grain whisky, which lacked the character we associate with Scotch today, turned easily to gin. Many found they preferred it, and this fresh loyalty was maintained after the war, when supplies returned to normal. Grain whisky was killed as a consumer product: the gainer was gin. Gin was also marginally cheaper than matured Scotch: in days when sixpence (2½p) difference in price really meant something, that, too, helped gin sales!

* * *

"When the clergyman's daughter
Drinks nothing but water,
She's certain to finish on gin."

Rudyard Kipling.

53

NOTES

1898 A CRUCIAL DEAL

It is idle to speculate whether, without this amalgamation Gordon's would have gone on to become the world leader in gin. Suffice it to say that the joining of the two companies was the most significant commercial step in London gin's modern development.

The new Tanqueray-Gordon company brought in as directors two Coombes (of Coombe's brewery) and a Mr. Serocold of Reid's, then renowned for their stout. The inclusion of brewers added to criticism in the licensed trade that the venture was quasi-monopolistic and it received some adverse press criticism, none of which had the slightest effect.

Charles Gordon the second lived to a year

after the amalgamation: amongst his inventions was a new breach-loading gun. The family connection survived only in the name and the boar's head trademark, first registered before the amalgamation and taken from the Gordon coat-of-arms.

I have employed Tanqueray and Gordon as particularly illustrative of the story of gin in England, or more particularly in London. Of other distillers from early days, Booth's was extremely influential, but it has in our own times declined in commercial importance. Comparatively new gin companies have enjoyed successes. However, they did not play major roles in the rise of gin from notoriety to eminence.

Gordon's moved steadily ahead after 1898, abroad as at home. Then, in January, 1920, came the closing of a market only just recovering from the dislocations of war – the U.S.A. (see chapter 10). Perhaps one should say, officially closed. In fact, much good London gin did find its way to the richer and more discerning American drinkers, and in the long run Prohibition was no bad thing in introducing gin to a wider spectrum of customers. (One old London distiller told me they had regrets about Repeal! In one instance, they sent, cash in advance, enormous consignments of gin to a remote island off the American coast whose handful of inhabitants would have found it hard to scrape up the money for a single bottle. Onward carriage was no concern of London's, though they had to fulfil instructions that packaging would be used that permitted each case of gin to float if cast into the ocean.)

On the ending of Prohibition in 1933, Gordon's were far advanced with plans to start distilling in the U.S.A., finally doing so at two centres. In fairly short order, Gordon's was number one American domestic gin. The same applies in many countries where it is made.

In the world at large, Gordon's is by far the best-known London dry gin, in its clear, brightly-labelled – and regrettably much imitated – bottle. First-time visitors to Britain may be disconcerted to find their gin in a dark green bottle, but that is far too well-established for it to be changed. Cosmopolitan folk are habituated to this seemingly strange packaging dichotomy which has harmed the brand not a jot.

As Gordon's gin went from strength to strength, Tanqueray waned in demand. Then, in 1950, came a major event in the modern story of gin. Tanqueray Special Dry was re-launched, in a new pack – which broke every "rule" in the liquor-marketing rubric! Tanqueray enjoyed a crescendo of demand until in 1985 it gained the position of number one imported gin in the U.S.A. and was granted a Queen's Award for export. It went on to successes in other prestige markets and the valuable "duty-free" trade.

The very distinctive Tanqueray bottle is said, I can't think why, to be modelled on a fire hydrant. It reminds me, much more appropriately, of a cocktail shaker. If the crest on the label intrigues you: it is not some designer's fancy. The crest was granted the English Tanquerays in 1738: the battle-axes recognise the part played in the Crusades by remote Tanqueray forebears. The heraldic pineapple comes from the coat-of-arms bestowed in 1767 on the ancient French Willaume family from whom the Tanquerays are descended.

Tanqueray Special Dry is distilled solely in London. It is a premium brand, normally sold at 47.3 per cent alcohol, well over normal strength for the U.K. The family association in Charles Tanqueray & Co. is maintained by John Tanqueray, great grandson of the founder, who directs the gin's global activities.

1915 A WAR BONUS

Measures affecting liquor under the Defence of the Realm Acts (cordially detested under the acronym DORA) lingered restrictively for many years. Even today, after the liberalisations of English regulations in 1988, some residual oddities of British licensing laws stem from 1914–18.

6

THE HEART OF THE MATTER

B.C. 430   YOUTH-GIVING ESSENCE

I admit that, amongst dates used in sub-headings, this one is put in to attract attention – yet not without some justification. About that time flourished Hippocrates, the Greek so-called Father of Medicine. Since primordial medication, as opposed to witchcraft, relied heavily on sound herbal potions, it is not too fanciful to believe that Hippocrates knew of the salubrious properties of oil of the juniper, which grew copiously in his country. One may be sure that the celebrated Roman doctor, Aurelius Cornelius Celsus (around A.D. 30) was familiar with juniper. He would have known it by the Latin *iuniperus* – "youth-producing". With virtual certainty we can say that the better-known Galen, working a century later, was conscious of juniper's virtues: its name alone denotes the high regard in which it was held in the ancient world.

Doubtless, *iuniperus* – with rare pedantry I avoid the "j" which came in much later – was in the repertoire of medieval physicians and did a lot more good than many items they employed. However, it was not until the 16th century that there is a record of juniper forming part of any beverage. This was a juniper-flavoured wine, said to have been invented by a son of Henry IV of France. It was known as "the wine of the poor", for reasons I have not discovered. The process would have added cost. Was it primarily a medicinal drink? Was it a means for improving a wine's keeping qualities? In a primitive way, the craft of distilling was fairly well-known, mainly as means of concentrating wine for distant transport. Could it have been that from this juniper-wine Protestant refugees from France in the early 16th century made a prototype "gin" that was perfected by Sylvius of Leyden and commercialised by the Dutch? (From his functions at the French Court, Theodore de Mayerne-Turquet (q.v.), later to found the Distillers Company of London, presumably would have met the inventive prince. One may speculate that he was aware of juniper-wine and the possibilities of distilling from it.)

For an exceedingly long time, juniper has been cherished for its healthy attributes. It is a vital constituent of gin.

* * *

PRODUCTION TODAY:

It is not the place to describe the principles of distillation. Our concern is with taking the purest, highly rectified neutral spirit (ethanol) and compounding it with certain wholesome flavourings in order to produce dry gin. This is in direct contrast to the production of whisky or cognac, of which the flavour is imparted by the malt or wine and from which unwanted congenerics must be permitted to dissolve during varied periods of maturation. The alcohol from which the best gins are made contains no displeasing congenerics. Flavouring is technically a congeneric: in the case of gin, these are all beneficent.

The base for most London gin is alcohol made from maize (corn), with a small proportion of barley sometimes. Such grain spirit is used for all important gin exported. Equally good spirit may be made from molasses and thus is widely used in gin for domestic U.K. consumption: so far as the consumer is concerned, there is no detectable difference in gin made to the same formula from either grain or cane spirit. "Grain" carries a certain prestige. In some countries other bases for neutral spirit are used – rice, dates, banana, grape, and so on – often with dire results. You cannot make good gin except from the purest spirit. This spirit, without any character, is totally boring – about as interesting as a glass of water. The magic wand of the gin rectifier and compounder transmogrifies it into a stimulating nectar.

Leading gin houses differ in particulars of production. But let us mention the principal ingredients. The first is, of course, juniper. This is widely grown, and buyers will move from market to market according to availability and price, both of which fluctuate yearly. A major gin firm will customarily hold two or three years supply of juniper. The berries come in dehydrated form, or they would go mouldy. They must be kept dry and are often stored in teak bins where they can be regularly raked to aerate them.

Big gin distillers, who need a large tonnage yearly, will take samples of juniper berries from a batch submitted and in their laboratory will exhaustively test them for oil content. They can thus calculate what percentage of the vital oil they will obtain per ton of the same crop: the yield and quality of oil from the juniper of a given country may vary greatly from year to year through climatic conditions. It is an increasingly costly commodity and careful purchasing pays.

The other prime ingredient of London dry gin is coriander seed. This looks rather like 'cow parsley' when growing: actually it belongs to the carrot family. It is widely farmed and does not share the market difficulties of juniper. The little fruits (seeds) have a delicate flavour reminding one of sage with a hint of lemon. Coriander also has many culinary applications. Other aromatics employed are calamus and angelica root, cassia and cinnamon bark, lemon and orange peel, and liquorice. All these natural ingredients are healthy or actively medicinal. Sometimes the quantities are proportionately very small, nor does every house use them all: other herbs may occasionally be included. The formulae for leading brands are closely guarded secrets. Though gin connoisseurs – the gintelligentsia to whom I shall refer – appreciate the subtle variations in dry gins, and have decided preferences – to say nothing of prejudices – there is a fallacious tendency to say they "are all the same." That is nonsense, or there would be little point to the expensive expertise involved in producing fine gin. One could dilate on elaborate procedures – there are several effective methods – but I think they were best condensed for me by the production director of one of London's great distilleries. I quote from a previous book of mine:

"Gin distillation is a batch process carried out in copper pot stills. After the required quantities of rectified spirit and botanical ingredients have been placed in the still, it is heated, usually be steam coils, to bring the contents to the boil. As the contents vaporize they are flavoured by the botanicals and in passing through a condenser change back to a liquid and become a gin distillate.

"The art of a gin distiller rests in controlling the rate of flow of the still and in determining which part of the distillate is suitable for the gin he is producing. In the initial stages of distillation, the output of the still is discarded [as too harsh]."

Like all condensations, that makes it all appear fairly simple: in reality it is rather complicated. Which is why there are few great gins; and many indifferent ones, made by short-cut processes from poor spirit that are reflected in their quality.

* * *

An American visitor – a member of the gintelligentsia – was being shown round the distillery that produced his favourite London dry gin, an establishment with which I was associated. He gazed admiringly at the great copper stills. He listened to his guide. He expressed astonishment at the vast gallonage of gin reposing in rows of huge vats. The tour ended, he was asked if he had any questions. "Yes," he answered. "Got an olive?"

NOTES

B.C. 430 YOUTH-GIVING ESSENCE

Hippocrates was a contemporary of Plato and Socrates. Many legends surround him, helped by his own claim to belong to a family founded by the mythical Aesculapius of Homer, later identified as the God of Healing. We owe the word diagnosis, in medical sense, to Hippocrates, and he may have invented the stethoscope. He believed in keeping the guts in good trim, so I bet he knew about juniper.

Celsus was a follower of Hippocratic principles. Not a great deal is known about this physician, who flourished around the reign of the Emperor Tiberius, though his surviving writings were required reading in medical schools in Europe into quite recent times.

More is known of Claudius Galen (131–*c.*200). He was against chemicals and pro-moted use of natural substances – such as juniper – in medicines. His theories held sway for many centuries. He was appointed by Marcus Aurelius as doctor to his son, the future Emperor Commodus (in power 180–192), whose dissolute reign heralded the final collapse of the Roman Empire. For his royal patient, Galen invented an appetiser – the first recorded "cocktail"? – of which the demented ruler thought highly. It consisted of (the natural substances) – wine, lemon juice and powdered adder, and was called Vini Gallici. Appropriately for anyone who could enjoy such a concoction, Commodus died by poisoning.

* * *

Junipers are conifers, of the cypress sub-order. There are numerous varieties, that associated with gin being *juniperus communis*

(the common juniper), widely found in Europe, north Asia and northern North America. Usually it is a shrub, though it may grow to 30 feet in ideal temperate conditions. The berries take two years to ripen: they are at their best just before fully ripe when they are rich in an aromatic oil that is lighter than water. It is wholly soluble in alcohol. The oil used also to be distilled from the twigs, when oil of juniper, bought from your friendly neighbourhood chemist, was a valued stimulant, sudorific (aiding perspiration) and diuretic (easing the work of your kidneys). These therapeutic benefits are thus mildly present in gin.

It has nothing to do with our subject, yet, with my love of digression and useless information, I cannot forebear to add that, when large enough, juniper wood is favoured in superior joinery. The bark was once made into rope; in Scotland, the roots were woven into rough baskets for vegetables. The wood was burned indoors as a precaution against cholera. Juniper berries were, and are, much used for pickling meat and other culinary purposes. Altogether a very valuable botanical specimen.

7

GREAT GIN DRINKS

A NAVAL OCCASION

H.M.S. Hercules (38 guns) wallowed on the oily swell off the Atlantic coast of South America, where the Essequibo river pushed into the ocean. To the South lay Demerara, re-named Georgetown. Twelve years previously, the territory of which it was the capital, captured from the French in 1796, had been formally ceded and would in future be called British Guiana.

The ship was attached to the West Indies station. Her commander had orders to watch out for any slave trader vessels: the trade itself was illegal though slavery had yet to be outlawed in the colonies. It had been an uneventful cruise and the crew had been allowed some shore leave, a welcome respite from the tedium of routine Caribbean patrols.

The ship's surgeon in Hercules, Henry Worksop, was popular with officers and ratings alike. A man of enquiring disposition, he was much interested in tropical fevers, and his ministrations probably accounted for the exceptional healthiness of the company. He was aware of the virtues of chinchona bark, or quinia, tincture of which had for some time been known as a specific against certain tropical disorders: the Admiralty had prescribed its regular use in His Majesty's ships in areas notorious for their fevers.

Ashore in Georgetown, Henry Worksop had been introduced by a local doctor to another medicinal bark, from the Angostura tree, named for a town in the former Spanish colony of Venezuela, now part of the republic of Gran Colombia. He had heard of this bark in England: He now discovered that it was traditionally used for beneficent infusions and had even been turned into commercial medicines by missionaries in order to provide extra funds to sustain their work. Worksop bought two jars of these medicinal "bitters". In the privacy of his tiny cabin – cubicle would be more descriptive – he set to analysing his newly-found compounds within the bounds of his limited pharmacological resources.

* * *

Deferentially, Henry Worksop said to his Captain, an officer of amiable disposition, "Instead of your customary daily draught, sir, I crave that you should try a fresh specific of my own concocting."

"Is it within regulations?" asked Captain Jack Bristow R.N. He came of a London family, with three generations of seafaring. He had been a gunnery lieutenant at Trafalgar and was looking forward eagerly to retirement, perhaps taking a minor part in the family business as wine and spirit merchants, if he could survive another year of this climate.

"Indeed it is in order, sir. It is my charge to seek any remedies, supplementary to those currently in use, that may help maintain the health of His Majesty's sailors. But that is not the sole reason for my request."

"Very well. I do not suppose you would wilfully poison me!" The Captain had quite a soft spot for the surgeon, who had brought him through a near fatal attack of unidentified ague.

Henry Worksop handed his commander a small glass containing a pale red fluid. "You need not toss it back as you would your dose of quinia, sir."

Captain Bristow tasted the drink suspiciously.

"It reminds me of – er, something."

"Of Hollands may I suggest sir."

"Indeed, Mr. Worksop. That is it, though it does not look like it. I often had Hollands in place of brandy or rum when we watched the Dutch coast in the anxious days when King William became sovereign of the Low Countries and just before Boney was defeated at Waterloo. I liked it well enough. But this tastes different, pleasantly so I think."

"Precisely so, sir. What I deem to be the salubrious essence of Angostura wood bark combines well with this spirit, which itself contains the excellent oil of juniper. I have tried it, sir, on some of your officers."

"I find it distinctly pleasing – mild and appetising."

"I have diluted it with a little water, sir, since ours is fresh from our last landfall."

"Watered, eh? Like the men's grog. Just as well perhaps, for the younger officers should they accept this invention of yours. See here, Mr. Worksop, in four days time it is His Majesty's birthday. I intend that you and all officers not on watch shall dine with me. It would be an amusing novelty if we were to start proceedings with a few tots of this – what'll we call it – this red gin of yours – if you can spare some."

"Most willingly, sir. But is not the gin, rather than red in hue, *pink?*"

1834   BAD VERSE, LONG LIFE

London man-about-town Algernon Bullstrode sauntered into the hotel owned by Mr. Limmer in Conduit Street, off Bond Street and close to fashionable Hanover Square, where Algernon lived as the pampered nephew of a rich aunt. He sprawled in a chair and picked up a copy of *The Times*, retaining his gloves so as not to soil his hands with ink. He rapped his cane on the table. "John!" he called loudly. The head-waiter heard him and came quickly.

"I'll have one of your best gin slings," he said, adding, to no one in particular, though a couple of men looked up with displeasure, "Too much portwine last night. Got a head as thick as one of Madame Tussaud's models," using for simile that French lady's newly fashionable waxworks of famous people. "Hello Bertie." He accosted a young man who had just come in. "Join me in a noggin."

"With great pleasure," said Bertie. He sat down, his tall hat still on his head. "I'll have whatever Mr. Bullstrode's drinking, John. I say, Algie, I've made up a jolly little rhyme about this place. Came to me while my man was shaving me this mornin'."

"Gawd, Bertie, not more of your tedious poetising."

Quite unoffended, for he was impervious to insults from those he considered to lack his own talent, Bertie took a slip of paper from his pocket. He opened a quizzing-glass, which was pure affection as his eyesight was sharper than his wits.

"Come on, let's get it over with," said Algernon.

Bertie cleared his throat, and read:

> "My name is John Collins, head waiter at Limmer's,
> Corner of Conduit Street, Hanover Square,
> My chief occupation is filling of brimmers
> For all the young gentlemen frequenters there."

Bertie waited for appreciation – in vain. In a corner, an elderly minor peer of the realm muttered audibly to his companion, "Noisy young pups." Algernon slowly clapped his gloved hands together in ironic applause.

"I suppose John may be flattered," he said. "His feeling for verse mercifully may not match his expertise in serving drinks, in which case he will not notice your execrable scansion."

"I think that to be immortalised in a poem is as grand a destiny as can befall a man," said Bertie, serenely content in his narcissistic egotism.

"Poem! Immortalise! Are you still drunk from last evening? I'd forget your ambition to be the new Lord Byron. Come on, let's stroll down to the club and see if we can rattle up a game of billiards. Poem! Oh, Gawd!" Algernon's cackling laughter rang loudly.

However, Bertie had the last, posthumous, laugh.

1857   SHARP'S THE WORD

As a senior official of the East India Company, James Jackson was accepted by the military as almost an equal, and Mrs. Jackson was more than accepted by their wives (few in number) for she lived much better than they did and employed at least twice the staff of the local army commander. It was this man, Major Sykes – something of a hero of the current mutiny of the sepoys and still recovering from wounds received at Agra – whom Mr. Jackson was entertaining to sundown refreshment on the verandah of his capacious bungalow. The troubles had entirely by-passed this tranquil hill station, whence Mr. Jackson, with growing inertia, administered a district almost as large as Wales. Indeed, so finely had he trained his underlings and native employees that he scarcely found it necessary to leave his home except for an annual visit to his superiors in distant Calcutta.

The specially trained servant, whom Mr. Jackson, who had a reputation as a wag, called his "drinks wallah", brought to the two men fresh glasses containing gin, freshly squeezed lime juice and a touch of sugar syrup, topped with water cooled in a gourd. It was one bearer's sole duty to keep these pottery-encased receptacles bathed in water as they hung in the sun, their contents being chilled by evaporation. It was not wholly effective, but ice was one luxury unobtainable here. As to gin, Mr. Jackson disdained that produced in Calcutta (with good reason) or the Hollands of sorts brought in from Batavia by Dutch traders. He could afford London distilled gin, imported in jars at considerable cost, transported hundreds of miles up river, on mule pack and finally on the backs of sweating porters.

"I must say, Jackson, you serve an uncommon pleasing peg. We usually have to do with the damned arak when we can't get a drop of decent whisky. I suspect our quartermaster sells most of our supplies on the sly."

"Yes, I am fortunate, Major. I do find gin the most acceptable spirit, particularly in the hot season. I used not to, but when I was last in London – five, six years ago – I was introduced to a gentleman who was a distiller. We got on very well and met a few times socially. Damme, eighteen months

later I received my first consignment of his gin – on credit. Now, every six or nine months, up it turns – less a few bottles broken or stolen – and I send back a draft on my London bankers. Worth every penny. They say some of our people are drinking gin with quinia in some form or other."

"Never heard of that. Thank God, we've got no malaria up here."

"I do like the astringency of this drink," said James Jackson, clapping his hands to attract the drinks-wallah. "We call it a gimlet."

"Gimlet?" queried the Major, who did not mind what it was called so long as there was more of it.

"Yes, Major – that carpenter's tool – sharp as a gimlet."

1865   THE GENERAL'S EXAMPLE

It was a glorious summer's day. Tunbridge Wells was at its best. Taking his morning constitutional stroll along the Pantiles, Lieut. General Sir

Archibald Rolfe-Smythson, K.C.S.I., was perfectly conscious of the polite stares and whispered comments that marked his stately progress. He raised his immaculate silk hat to the few persons he recognised: it had only been six weeks since he moved into his splendid villa on the outskirts of the fashionable Kentish spa. He had been fortunate in India: honours, preferment and enrichment had not ravaged him with the usual concomitant sickness. He had emerged honourably from the Mutiny without a scratch and with some glory. He had, following the reorganisation of Indian government in 1858, been rewarded with posts of increasing prestige in splendid locations, whereas he had seen many a worthy colleague into early graves. It would have been churlish to refuse the occasional handful of jewels presented by a grateful maharajah, compensations for rare dangers and discomforts.

Sir Archibald signalled with his thick rattan walking-stick, its gold handle fashioned as a crouching tiger with ruby eyes, and the open carriage that had followed him at a discreet distance drew up beside him. It conveyed him to his home, re-named Durbar Hall. He lived there alone. Lady Rolfe-Smythson had barely survived to be so called before succumbing to some undiagnosed fever: she had never been robust. Their three sickly children had all predeceased her. Sir Archibald had every intention of remarrying: he was, after all, but fifty-five years old. This time it would not be the younger daughter of an interbred old county family but a sensible young widow of sound breeding, of which he had already perceived there was no shortage in the little town.

He had invited to luncheon – no longer tiffin – two of his more immediate neighbours, the Dixons and Murdocks. Mr. Dixon was "in trade", though you would not notice it until told; Dr. Murdock was the best-known, if far from the best, doctor in a place prolific in competing medical practitioners. Their wives were, in Sir Archibald's opinion, of no consequence, although Mrs. Murdock was distantly related to a Lady-in-Waiting to the Queen, a fact of which no one could long fail to be aware in her presence. Before luncheon, the ladies were offered Madeira wine.

"I wonder, gentlemen, if you would prefer to join me in what I refer to as my medicine – though I assure you I need no such thing, doctor." Mr. Dixon and Dr. Murdock instantly accepted. Sir Archibald had, as was customary, brought home from his imperial career two Indian servants. Robed in white, with sparklingly crisp turbans, these dignified men had silently served the ladies and then placed in front of Sir Archibald a Benares brass tray. It stood on a table composed of mounted elephants' feet, which excited great interest from the two ladies. "Shot it myself," said the General. "And that tiger, and that buffalo." He gestured towards a wall where the preserved heads of many a victim calmly observed their slayer's festivities.

The tray held three stout tumblers, a decanter, and a bowl of ice in which was imbedded a sealed bottle of liquid with the faintest blue tinge to it.

"Is not that what is referred to as Indian quinine water?" said Dr. Murdock.

"You are correct, sir. And I have had not a little trouble in obtaining it since my return for I understand it is not used in this country, which, since it is a British invention, may seem a trifle odd. You have not tasted it?"

"Not in such a form," said the doctor. "I am, of course, familiar with quinine."

"So am I, Dr. Murdock, and very nasty stuff it is. Which is why someone, perhaps a medical officer, suggested we take it with gin. It goes ill with other spirits. Yet it did not become something one could take with pleasure until quinine-water was invented. I suppose it is really just quinine tincture dissolved in selzter, maybe sweetened a little. Anyways, it caught on with us and we'd call it our "tonic." One or two chemists are now making it. I have had some from the people who took over from that Mr. Schweppe of Bristol."

"Do you think, sir, that it might take on in this country?" asked Mr. Dixon, whose commercial instinct had raised him from fairly obscure beginnings to a decent position in society.

"Very low incidence of malaria in England," said the doctor.

"I was thinking of it as a social beverage, with medicinal undertones," said Mr. Dixon. "Though, saving your presence General, gin does not enjoy a high reputation among the better sort of people – at least not in Tunbridge."

"Gin is, however, a healthful spirit," countered Dr. Murdock, "provided it be not made by some doubtful methods."

"I buy direct from the best sources," said the General.

"Pardon me, sir, I would not dream of suggesting otherwise. I have rarely tasted it before. I was repeating what I had heard about certain aspects of the trade. I say, however, without equivocation, that taken like this it is a singularly pleasant and refreshing drink. Don't you say so, Dixon?"

"I do; quite delicious."

"We have left the ladies unattended too long," said the General.

* * *

It was not long afterwards that Dr. Murdock was entertaining a few male friends in his library after a meeting of a local body concerned with amateurs of Tunbridge Wells ware.

"Good Lord, Murdock you taken to old Mother's Ruin?" exclaimed Major Grampian, jovially enough, as he saw the decanter of clear spirit.

"Have you never drunk gin with Indian quinine water?" asked the doctor, with a distinct tone of superiority.

"Never served in India," said Major Grampian, who had spent most of his undistinguished career in Aldershot or minor overseas garrisons. Dr. Murdock handed a gin and "tonic" to each man.

"It is there often referred to as 'tonic'," said Dr. Murdock, implying an intimate knowledge of the sub-continent, though in fact he had never been further abroad than Paris, and there only once (terrible drains). "Gin and 'tonic' water is a great favourite with Sir Archibald Rolfe-Smythson," he added. His friends were impressed for they had yet to meet the town's newest celebrity.

"Mrs. Grampian takes a gin – for her health you know – but I had never thought of it as a drink for gentlemen. But if Sir Archibald . . ." his voice trailed off.

"Oh, I've had an occasional gin sling in London," put in Leonard Crimp, who was known to be "something in the City": one did not enquire what, but it evidently was lucrative and entailed him going there four days a week by the railway. "I assure you gin is quite the thing. I shall ask in my club if they have this quinine water or whatever. I think it's a damned fine drink."

"Dixon's pharmacy has a supply. He obtained it specially for Sir Archibald."

"I shall order some at once," said the Major. "Should he call on us, it would be deplorable if we had none at home."

"I dare say he'll get round to your place – eventually," said Dr. Murdock. "May I re-fill your glass – or would you prefer something else?"

"Oh, no," said Major Grampian "Another gin and – er tonic water would suit me admirably."

1890   A WARM TIME IN WASHINGTON

Washington, DC, virtually closed down in high summer, Politicians, and the Society that battened on them, were vacationing at Saratoga Springs, or had taken conveyances, ranging from private railcars to other people's buggies, to the Atlantic coast, to the hills, to anywhere outside the steamy Potomac valley. So Joe was annoyed that he had had to leave the tree-shaded lawns around a newly-rich industrialist's Long Island mansion (his "holiday cottage") for the hell of a Washington hotel suite. But business was business, and even at this season there were perspiring palms to grease in the federal capital and urgent conversations to be held that one did not wish to confide to the crackling wires of the Edison Telephone Company.

Joe, hot and thirsty, entered Shoemaker's Bar, crowded when Congress was in session but now almost deserted.

"Mornin', colonel," the barkeep greeted him. "What'll be the colonel's pleasure this sunny day?"

Now Joe Rickey was not a proper colonel: he was one by self-promotion and would not have known what to do with a rifle except to shoot someone in the back with it.

"I'll have my usual," said Joe, fanning himself with his broad-brimmed hat. "When have you heard me ask otherwise?"

"Can't say – but I ain't bin here that long, Colonel Jim." If anyone knew why Joe was always called Jim, and not by his baptismal forename (presuming he had ever been baptised), they had forgotten the reason. He was Colonel Jim Rickey, the lobbyist, retained by some of the largest concerns in the United States, whose secrets he would take to his grave – so long as the fees were forthcoming.

Colonel Jim watched as the barkeep made up the drink which had first

been evolved in the bar for the Colonel years before. He cut in half a lime, squeezed the juice over ice chips in a tumbler and tossed in the crushed rind, poured on top a generous measure of gin, gave the mix a brief stir and ended with a squirt of club-soda. He placed the finished drink in front of his sweating customer.

"Half the Congressmen who come here order a Rickey," he said with gross exaggeration: a little flattery helped the tip.

"I'd as soon they asked for me personally," answered Colonel Jim.

1912   CLASSIC OF CLASSICS

Luigi thanked all the Saints in the calendar for his ever arriving in the United States. He had hoped to work his passage in a great new liner on her maiden voyage. Unforeseen circumstances had prevented his joining her: on that fateful April night in the Atlantic, she had sunk with huge loss of life. Failing to get on to Titanic, Luigi had sailed later in the year: now he was a junior aide to his countryman, Martini di Arma di Taggia, head bartender at the fashionable Knickerbocker Hotel, New York City.

Luigi watched signor Martini as closely as his humble duties permitted, intent on one day becoming a bartender himself. He was destined so to be, ending his distinguished career as what may be described as bartender emeritus, manager of the bar at the Savoia Majestic in Genoa, which city was also the last resting place of Martini. But now, as a youth, he was only an observer as Martini personally attended to the whims of the rich and famous. Amongst regular clients was that great hero of all Italians, the opera star of stars, Caruso: he disdained the cocktails that were becoming the vogue and stuck to vintage French champagne. On the other hand, John D. Rockefeller, the alternatively reviled and respected oil tycoon, was fond of a special mix peculiar to the Knickerbocker. Its growing band of influential devotees called it by the name of the popular bartender who had evolved it a year or so previously; they called it the Dry Martini. It was considered much superior to other "martini" cocktails or to the old sweet Martinez invented by the celebrated Jerry Thomas, with which the Dry Martini was later sometimes to be erroneously linked. Signor Martini's Knickerbocker mix was half-and-half imported London dry gin and French (Noilly Prat) vermouth, with a touch of orange bitters. Apart from the bitters, what Martini did that made his so different from the simple gin-and-French was that he stirred the ingredients with lots of ice in a mixing-glass and then strained the drink into a chilled cocktail glass. Some innovative customers took to spearing a green olive with a cocktail stick and putting it into their glass, a habit which bartenders later adopted. An alternative, or addition, was a zest of lemon peel: the peel was eventually largely to supersede the olive. (Today, some Martinians like the zest squeezed over the glass but not immersed.)

The ever attentive Luigi noted that Mr. Rockefeller, whose alleged stinginess was a legend he cultivated and which was publicised in the press, must have been impressed by Martini's expertise, for he always left a substantial tip – 25 cents.

By the time Luigi left the Knickerbocker to pursue his own life as bartender to the international set, the Dry Martini was established as the smartest of cocktails, the preferred one in a thousand bars – to say nothing of homes (and speakeasies for that matter). Twenty years after Martini made the first one, the Dry Martini reigned supreme internationally as the aperitif mix of the sophisticated world. But the *ultra*-dry Martini had yet to come.

1925   SWEET AND LOVELY LADY

E rnest Hemingway was aware of his own genius, and also conscious that its flame was not burning with the intensity of his slightly older friend, Francis Scott Fitzgerald – before they quarrelled. The latter's *Tender is the Night* had enjoyed considerable acclaim the year before and in this year he was to publish *The Great Gatsby*. Earnest hoped for similar success from his (now forgotten) *Torrents Of Spring*, though his guide and mentor, Maxwell Perkins, told him Scribner's were only taking it to obtain the more promising *The Sun Also Rises*. As usual, Perkins was right.

Ernest and Scott had lunched that day in Montparnasse with Christian Gauss. They argued over following Robert Louis (*Treasure Island*) Stevenson's advice that a young author should always copy his seniors in the craft until a style of his own developed. They had disagreed.

"I'm meeting Zelda at Harry's," said Scott. "Let's stroll across the river." Hemingway was living in Paris: the Fitzgeralds, new darlings of the Jazz Age, were on a visit, not wholly unconnected with escape from an America wracked by the tribulations of Prohibition.

The two young men took their time, dallying at the bookstalls lining the *quais* beside the Seine. They did not reach Harry's New York Bar, in narrow rue Danou, until around tea-time – not that Harry's served tea. Harry's was fashionable with a section of the expatriate Anglo-American literary set, though others would go thirsty rather than be seen there: it was in a smart part of the *rive droite* – far removed from what they deemed artistic Paris. On their way, Ernest and Scott passed the Ritz, whose bar was, in days of affluence, to become a favourite with Ernest: indeed he was to "liberate" it many years later!

Zelda had already arrived at the bar in rue Danou. She was talking animatedly to a couple of American tourists.

"At last, Scott!" she said. "Do you like my new hat? It cost a fraction of what it would on Fifth Avenue."

"Very much," replied Scott, kissing her cheek. She was slightly intoxicated but, so far, attractively. "You know Ernest, of course."

"You know I do," said Zelda, a trifle resentful of anybody she thought a potential rival to her brilliant husband.

"I'll have another White Lady," said Zelda, ignoring her erstwhile companions whom she made no effort to introduce. Scott, ever well-mannered, nodded to them with a smile and a faint shrug. They smiled back and soon left.

"What's a White Lady?" asked Scott.

"Oh, it's a lovely cocktail, brand new, they've just invented it here – specially for me! You wouldn't like it – it's sweet and delicious."

"Then I'll have a White Lady, too – for you are sweet and delicious."

Ernest Hemingway was vaguely repelled by the sentimentality of the remark. "A Martini for me," he said, "and distinctly dry."

1928   CHARLEY COMES UP TRUMPS

After initial anxieties, Prohibition had little impact for the hard-drinking members of the Bohemian club, The Players', in New York City. They were congenitally the sort of people – actors, writers, artists – who would be reluctant to allow a federal aberration to upset their routine. The committee came up with an ingenious solution: they closed the club's bar in accordance with the law, and it was given to Charley Connolly, the bartender, who was to run it as he cared to and keep any profit. So The Players' became an exclusive speakeasy.

It was during this (for some) arid period that Charles Dana Gibson, the famous American artist and originator of the Gibson Girl, came into the club in indecisive mood.

"I don't quite know what I want, Charley." He thought for a few moments. "Charley, make me a *better* Martini."

How could he make a better Martini, thought Charley, than the ones members already considered perfect? So he prepared the cocktail in his usual way, and then placed a pearl onion on a cocktail stick and immersed it in the frosted glass. He presented it to the artist.

"Looks nicer than an olive," said Charles Dana. He swizzled the little impaled vegetable around and then ate it. "Improves the onion." He sipped the drink.

"Can't say it's *better* Charley. A bit different though. I think I'll always have mine this way."

"I'll call it the Gibson," said Charley.

It soon got around that Charles Dana was drinking a new cocktail. It was not really new: it just looked new. Members, by nature gossipy, soon spread the word around in circles avid for any novelty. In no time at all, celebrities, or those who thought they were celebrities, were asking for Gibsons in their own favourite speakeasies.

* * *

"I must get out of these wet clothes, and into a dry Martini."

– attributed to Alexander Woolcott.

NOTES

1826 A NAVAL OCCASION

The origin of Pink Gin has been a matter for dispute. I propounded a naval provenance during an exchange of letters in the correspondence columns of the *Daily Telegraph* some years ago: no one authoritatively contradicted the theory. Undeniably, at an uncertain date, Pink Gin became the traditional drink of Royal Navy officers. The drink was usually made with Plymouth gin, because of the long naval association with that city, until World War II (see Chapter 13).

From a heavily bittered social-cum-medicinal potion, it may be assumed that the mix was refined over the years and that retired naval men brought the Pink Gin habit ashore with them and into their retirement. Their use of gin must have been a potent factor in gin's rise to respectability.

* * *

By far the best-known and most widely distributed aromatic bitters are Angostura. The word is the registered trademark of the company founded in the eponymous town by Dr. Siegert in 1825: Siegert was a veteran medical officer of the Prussian army. The town of Angostura was later re-named Ciudad Bolivar, and a considerable time ago production of the bitters was moved to Trinidad, where it continues with Siegerts still on the board of the company. We have every reason to believe that Angostura bitters today are substantially the same as the product discovered by our fictional Henry Worksop, for by then Dr. Siegert had perfected his refinement of local preparations and was selling it.

* * *

Pink Gin is made by splashing some drops of Angostura into a glass and shaking out any surplus, so that the inside is lightly coated

with the bitters. Add a couple of measures of gin, ice if you like, and dilute with plain or charged water to taste. There was once a fad for using a warmed glass and setting fire to the bitters (which are strongly alcoholic) before dousing it with gin – a peculiarly pointless gimmick, making an acrid drink, which I have not seen perpetrated in modern times. Pink Gin is a peculiarly sane aperitif drink.

A touch of Angostura may with advantage be added to a gin-and-tonic, if the tonic-water be on the sweet side (as some makes are).

1834 BAD VERSE, LONG LIFE

The verse – by that prolific author, Anon – is more quoted than its quality justifies. It has long outlived Limmer's Hotel. And so John Collins was immortalised. In sundry forms, the Collins became one of the enduring gin mixes – and spawned many egregious mutations, with other spirits. In circles where esoteric details of mixology are discussed – and such exist – there has been disputation as to whether there is a difference between a John and a Tom Collins. The oldest recipe book I have (1882) says a John Collins is made with Hollands gin and a Tom Collins with Old Tom ("genuine only"). As neither types are used in cocktails today, the question is purely academic. Some aver that whatever the drink was that made Limmer's famous in its day, "John" came to be corrupted to "gin", which was why a Collins was made with gin. In effect, a Collins is a Gin Sling. Sling derives from *schlingen* (to swallow): it was well established in English usage in the early 19th century. In her *One Shilling Cookery Book*, Mrs. Isabella Mary Beeton (1835–65) gives a recipe for a Gin Sling, a strong indication of gin's acceptance in the genteel households for whose guidance she wrote.

Mrs. Beeton's recipe:
Ingredients – 1 wineglassful of gin, 2 slices of lemon, 3 lumps of sugar, ice.
Mode – Put the gin, sugar and sliced lemon into a tumbler and fill up with small pieces of ice or iced-water. Drink through a straw.
Average cost – 3d. [= 1.25p!]

General modern recipe for a gin Collins:
2 measures dry gin
2 teaspoons each lemon juice and caster sugar,
Dash of Angostura (optional),
Mix in tumbler with ice cubes and top with soda-water.

A Gin Fizz is similar in ingredients, but they are shaken and strained into a glass before adding the soda-water.

Other drinks fall broadly into the Collins/ Sling category, such as the Singapore Gin Sling and the Clover Club: see chapter 10 – recipes.

1857 SHARP'S THE WORD

The Gimlet is certainly a legacy from the old British Empire; which part of it is problematical. It is a less sharp drink today, but a refreshing one:

Shake vigorously 2 measures each gin and Rose's lime juice cordial. Strain into suitable glass (on-the-rocks if you like), adding soda-water at personal discretion. For a tarter version, add some fresh lime or lemon juice to the Rose's.

A gin-and-lime is a satisfactory long drink; no shaking, but it is not a Gimlet. There is no satisfactory substitute for Rose's cordial.

1865 THE GENERAL'S EXAMPLE

Arguably, the most important gin mix today is gin-and-tonic (water). Indisputably, the introduction of tonic-water to the British social scene did as much to spread the use of gin as any single development.

Sir Archibald Rolfe-Smythson is used to typify the type of imperial proconsul who inadvertently helped to popularise gin.

The end of the 18th century saw the production of artificial "spa" waters as a practical commercial proposition. Though heavily taxed as a patent medicine, bottled soda-water was so successful that its pioneer in Britain – Jacob Schweppe – was able to retire in 1799. From carbonated "spa" water it was a short step to incorporating other ingredients and botanicals. Obviously, there would be a demand for an additive containing quinine for sale in those climes where quinine was regularly used medicinally. Gradually, the quinine content was reduced – as it has again been in our own era – and the sugar increased: there are sugar-free tonic-waters, though many people do not care for them. The modern spin-off from tonic-water, bitter-lemon (which is not really bitter at all) is fairly popular in Britain, which has a "sweet tooth" nationally. In some countries "tonic" may not be used to describe (Indian) quinine water: quite widely, Schweppes has become a synonym for the product.

1890 A WARM TIME IN WASHINGTON

There really was a Colonel Jim, lobbyist, who frequented this bar: the Rickey was named for him. Originally, a Gin Rickey was based on Hollands or Old Tom gin. Using dry gin today, one would always add a little grenadine syrup to the Shoemaker recipe given above.

1912 CLASSIC OF CLASSICS

Luigi was a real person and his story a true one, based on a recording of him made in the nineteen-sixties at the Savoia Majestic by my friend and ardent Martinian, James Porter. The tape itself has been lost, but not before I had noted all the details (including the mention of John D. Rockefeller), which I first published in 1971. I am flattered that my story is being increasingly accepted as representing the true origin of the Dry Martini, superseding sundry notions and unwarranted assumptions. It is sometimes thought that the cocktail gets its name from the eponymous vermouth. It could not, for Martini & Rossi did not produce dry vermouth at that time, though they were to become leaders in that style later and eventually acquired Noilly Prat as well.

* * *

The Dry Martini has retained its prestige, its aura of sophistication, its strange mystique. Yet, in our own age, it has suffered from its virtues. It is simple in an epoch which likes the complicated, dry when the vogue is for creamy sweet cocktails, flavoursome in the era of the bland, and powerful at a time when low alcohol content is prized. It is no longer the fashion to enjoy a Three Martini Lunch – or even to enjoy lunch at all. Where Martinis once revived laggard spirits, relaxed tensions, heightened wit and sharpened appetite, now pallid coolers of wine

and juices or fizzy waters, clammily try to stimulate pre-prandial conversation.

Maybe the decline of the Dry Martini started with the dilutive effect of serving it "on-the-rocks", or the innovation of the vodkatini, mutation of the original characterful gin version. There were other and mostly lamentable deviations from the traditional mix: amongst the weirdest was substitution of Chanel No. 5 for vermouth. Only one small variation deserves attention: see 1928 (Notes) hereafter.

Has the true Martini, which I deservedly have titled "the classic of classics", passed into history, its legends more potent than its actuality? I do not think so. It is still alive, its merry flame guarded by an elite brotherhood of drinkers. When, inevitably, the wheel of fashion returns from the weak and boring to the robust and tasteful, the wonderful "straight up" Dry Martini will resume its rule over the fabulous world of cocktails.

* * *

The extent to which the delicate simplicity of the Dry Martini has been contaminated by complication is illustrated by the 268 "Martinis" listed in *The Perfect Martini Book* (a misnomer in my opinion) by Robert Herzbrun. I could add further versions if I wished to – which I emphatically do not. I dealt with many a legend, and invented not a few, in my own *Stirred, Not Shaken*, which claimed to be the first proper book wholly devoted to this cocktail. For those who wish to pursue their studies in greater historic and literary depth, there is Prof. Lowell Edmunds' remarkable *The Silver Bullet – The Martini in American civilization*: a masterpiece of research and entertaining erudition.

To be provocative – since every Martini fan has his or her individual quirks, preferences and prejudices – I will didactically present my own recipe:

Pre-chill required number of stemmed 5 ozs (125 ml) glasses.

bitters archaic. Even with a large mixing-glass, it is undesirable to make more than four servings at one time.

*   *   *

On Martinis:

H. L. Mencken – "The only American invention as perfect as a sonnet."

Bernard DeVoto – "The supreme American gift to world culture."

Nikita Khrushchev – "The U.S.A.'s most lethal weapon."

1925 SWEET AND LOVELY LADY

Harry's New York Bar, Paris:

This was opened in 1911, arguably the first truly American watering-hole outside the U.S.A. The International Bar Flies club was founded there in 1924, its members being serious topers who were mostly well-heeled fugitives from Prohibition. Into the 'thirties Harry's retained much of its original ambience, though increasingly invaded by gawping tourists hoping to see the literary lions who had long deserted it for other zoos. Though physically little altered, nowadays it is quite fashionable with young French business executives; also a resort of the richer hippies. Old-timers like myself tend to avoid it: I pay a nostalgic visit about every other year, though I know I am going to be disappointed.

White Lady:

This famous and delightful cocktail was certainly evolved in Harry's in the 'twenties, though that it was made for Zelda Fitzgerald is entirely apocryphal: it is just the sort of thing that might have happened. (The luncheon mentioned is a matter of record.)

Half-fill substantial mixing-glass with clean ice cubes.

Pour in 3 measures Martini Extra Dry vermouth.

Strain off and discard the vermouth.

Pour over the vermouth-flavoured ice 3 measures Tanqueray or Gordon's gin per serving.

Stir briskly for 15 seconds.

Strain immediately into prepared glasses.

Squeeze firmly over each glass a slice of lemon peel.

Then get ready to repeat the performance.

N.B. If re-using same ice, for second round, be sure any water from melting is discarded. Glasses should not be filled to brim: regular Martinians hands are not always that steady. Peel from the (washed) lemon not to be immersed in the cocktail: immersion is a religious not a bar ritual. An olive is an intrusion and the use of orange

Classic recipe:

2 measures dry gin.

1 measure each of lemon juice and Cointreau.

teaspoon egg white.

Shake vigorously and strain into large cocktail glass.

Some modern books omit egg white: I say it is essential.

Hemingway:

Though he became fond of Daiquiris during his long Cuban residence, Hemingway was really a Martini man, often having his fictional characters drinking them. In "The Sun Also Rises", a key scene towards the conclusion involved an almost ritual drinking of Martinis.

The reference to Hemingway "liberating" the Ritz Bar (rue Cambon) concerns his arrival in Paris in 1944 amongst the first wave of Allied troops and war correspondents. He made straight for the bar and set up an unofficial "headquarters" there.

Ritzy digression:

Immediately post-war, the Ritz was the only place in Paris where you could rely on getting imported London dry gin. I queried how it came about that they were using gin bottled before 1940: it was House of Lords gin, the labels of which used to be dated. It transpired that the rich old Ritz used to make a practice of ordering in quantities sufficient to last three years. In 1939, before war broke out, they had bought a huge consignment of various drinks, and before the Germans occupied Paris had secreted a vast cache, which was never discovered, on the outskirts of the city. Foresight and luck paid handsome dividends. They were charging astronomic prices for their Martinis: I paid willingly.

1928 CHARLEY COMES UP TRUMPS

This has only peripheral bearing on gin, and I could have included it in earlier sections, yet it is an attractive true anecdote, expanded from information given to me, in the Players' Club itself, by the writer and drink specialist John McCarthy, of Rye, N.Y.

When Prohibition's sinister grip was unclasped in 1933, Charley Connolly, now much enriched by the years of drought – the law never laid a finger on him – quietly handed the bar back to the committee and resumed his place as club steward. He died some 15 years ago.

For a long time the Gibson was the only acceptable variation on the classic Martini. Martinian purists who disapproved of it caustically called it A.O.S. (Alcoholic Onion Soup).

8

*W*HY *C*OCKTAILS?

1989 FABLES, MYTHS AND LEGENDS

*T*he lasting, if variable, vogue for cocktails owes a great deal to gin. Conversely, gin is much indebted to cocktails. All spirits have some cocktails based on them: none is more suitable than gin – dry gin – for it blends perfectly with most other things, has an elusive character to impart. It is in itself an addition to a drink, not merely a means of alcoholising a soft concoction. Thus cocktails – I use the term very broadly to cover mixed drinks – are highly germane to our main topic.

What is the origin of the very odd word Cocktail? In Thackeray's day it was used to describe a fop: "Such a coxcomb as that, such a cocktail," he wrote, describing a man. But that was long after the word was also used for a mixed drink. The Oxford English Dictionary defines Cocktail, inter alia, as "a drink made of spirit, bitters, some sugar, etc. Chiefly U.S., 1809." This refers to the first known written mention of cocktail, in a potable sense, in an American journal. But etymological detail is absent. No wonder folk tales thrive.

*P*lease imagine nine men sitting in my home. They are members of the National Institute of Ginocologists, better known by the acronym NIG, an extremely exclusive organisation. I have brought them together to discuss "Cocktail", in the context of this book.

First James Darlington:

"My favourite story of the cocktail's origin is the one given by the great Harry Craddock, the American who made the bar of the Savoy hotel, in London, into a mecca for the rich and famous. His notion was printed in his *Savoy Cocktail Book*, the first important British publication of its type, published in 1930. I have a rare first edition."

"James," I interrupted, "we are not the least concerned with the contents of your library. Get on with it."

"Harry Craddock gave it as, and I quote, 'The true and uncontrovertible story of the origin of the Cocktail'."

"Which I shall doubtless *con*trovert shortly," put in David Jermyn, but James was not to be put off and continued,

"It goes like this. Around the early part of the last century, there was considerable trouble between the United States and Mexico."

"Remember the Alamo!" murmured Al Koole, who hails from Texas though now a London resident.

"We really must have quiet," I said. "Go on James."

"Craddock says that the king of Mexico held a parley with an American general to discuss peace terms. When they were all seated, before proceedings began, the king asked the Americans if they would like some refreshment. Naturally, the general said Yes, through politeness and because it was darned hot in that tent. So the king clapped his hands and a stunning girl came in with a great golden cup, but no one would drink first – a question of confusion on etiquette. The girl gets impatient, so what does she do? She drinks whatever's in that chalice. Everyone laughs, though it's not a laughing matter for all the booze has gone. But the girl's action has broken the ice and a truce is patched up for the time being. Before he left, the general asks the king who the splendid girl is. 'Oh, she's my daughter,' says he. 'Her name is Xcoctl'."

"Cocktail, eh?" says the general, typically no linguist. "I'll see to it that her name isn't forgotten."

* * *

"What a silly tale," said David Jermyn. "There weren't any Mexican kings, not after independence. They just had presidents, for assassination purposes, an occasional emperor to depose and execute, and the odd dictator. And, anyway, the word cocktail was already in use."

"There's another version of James's anecdote," I said. "It relates that an American admiral was paying a visit to a local Mexican overlord. All the visitors were offered a delicious concoction made and served by the chief's lovely daughter. He said her name was something that sounded like Cocktail, and the American said he'd ensure it was immortalised."

"Fairy tales," insisted David.

"Well, tell us the story you fancy," I said.

* * *

"I much prefer the one about Betsy Flanagan. It was written by Fenimore Cooper, the *Last of the Mohicans* chap. During the War of Independence Betsy ran a tavern in Yorktown, much frequented by General Washington's officers and also by some of Lafayette's French volunteers. Betsy kept chickens, but much finer ones were owned by a neighbour who was suspected of being a supporter of King George. Goaded by hurt pride and patriotism, one night Betsy purloined a few of these birds which she considered forfeit to the new state. She served these chickens at a feast for her military customers, and, to signalise her triumph, decorated with the fowls' tail feathers the flagons of drink on the festive board. This mystified her guests until she explained that they represented her little victory over her dubious neighbour. As the evening progressed and all manner of drinks were imbibed, the Frenchmen not only drank many toasts to the Republic but, in honour of Betsy's culinary enterprise and to show their growing

knowledge of her language, cried Vive le Cock-tail. So cocktail came to apply to a general mixing of drinks, before becoming more specific."

"That's a load of tripe," said James, "and much less romantic than my Mexican princess."

* * *

"Mine's a Revolutionary war story, too," said Charles St. J. Crichton. "It also concerns a tavern, of which the ardently pro-Washington landlord had given his hero's name to his champion fighting cock. Now his daughter Bessie – not Betsy – was in love with an American soldier. However, though admiring the young man's valour, the innkeeper thought him too lacking in worldly goods to make a fit suitor and declared marriage out of the question. Then Washington, the cock, disappeared. The distraught owner said he would offer the reward of his daughter to the man finding it: he does not appear to have covered the possibility of a woman being the discoverer. Surprise, surprise! In short order, Bessie's soldier boy turns up with the missing bird. The landlord said he would keep his word and a betrothal banquet was arranged. Bessie got over-excited and, when preparing lavish drinks for the occasion, produced some strange mixtures. The assembly found them very stimulating and, knowing the background story of the cock-napping, dubbed them 'cock-tails'. The description gained currency in other taverns and passed into daily speech."

* * *

"I've got a much more likely theory, which also happens to be connected with cock-fighting." This from my old friend Harry Kovaire "Two connecting theories, in fact."

"You mean in myth," interpolated David.

"Do shut up," I said. "You've had your turn. We're not in the House of Commons, so let's hear each other quietly."

"In the eighteenth century," continued Harry, "it was customary to dose cocks, just before a fight, with spirituous mixtures in order further to inflame their aggressiveness. This was called cock-ale. The inference is obvious. Another related idea is that cocktail derives from the custom, after a cock-fight, of toasting a victorious bird in a drink containing as many ingredients as it had remaining tail feathers. Hence, such a drink was called a cock-tail."

We all quite approved of that one. Harry was unable to remember where he got his notions. I think he read them in a book I once wrote – but I can't recall where I got them from either: so I kept silent.

* * *

Monty Duchaine has claimed a totally unsubstantiated French ancestry: his intimates know his father altered the family name from Chain, but they do not begrudge his little conceit. Typically, there was a Gallic flavour to his contribution:

"There was this French physician in New Orleans – well after the Louisiana Purchase I would think – who was noted for his inventive

hospitality. He made marvellous mixed drinks, but he had an eccentricity –
or _egg_centricity – of serving them in those double eggcups they use in France,
called _coquetiers_. His American friends couldn't quite get their tongues
round that – or not after they'd had a few – so they called them cocktails."

"Oh, God – this is getting worse," said David, who was becoming a bit
tight.

"Do shut up," I repeated.

* * *

"I'll give you another French tale." This from Jay Dee. "And a more likely
one. It also comes from the American War of Independence. There was a
very old sort of wine-based mixed drink once popular in Bordeaux – no
particular recipe it seems – called _coquetel_. It may have started as a
reinforcement for indifferent wine. Some of Lafayette's officers amused
their American counterparts by blending wine and spirits and so on. Asked
what it was, the French replied _'Coquetel'_, which was easily Americanised as
cocktail and became transferred to mixed drinks in general."

That got mutters of approval, as I circulated a bottle appropriately labelled
"The heart of a good cocktail."

* * *

"I'll intrude the absurd once more," said Al. "Don't drown it!" he barked
at me amicably as I poured some iced Malvern water into his glass. "I think
this story was given an airing in an early edition of the United Kingdom
Bartenders' Guild's international guide. We return for this to Mexico, to the
Gulf – but no fair maidens this time. Rather, a sleazy bar at Campeche,
popular a century and a half ago with American and Limey sailors. They
loved the powerful punches that were a speciality of the barkeeper who used
to stir his mixes with a peculiarly shaped root. This was known locally as _cola
de gallo_, which translates as 'cock's tail' – and so . . ."

"Spare us!" somebody muttered.

* * *

"There is something undeniably entrancing about old-time Mississippi
stern-wheel paddle-steamers," commenced John Bradley Hutton, who
tends to an orotund approach to anecdotes. "There is an enticing aura of
glamour in prints, contemporary writings, which lingers – though I doubt if
much of it was once apparent to the average passenger hoping to get from St.
Louis to New Orleans without disaster."

"Oh, do get on with it," said David, about whose continued membership of NIG I was beginning to entertain doubts.

"Now it appears that on the great river steamers, a successful gambler would sometimes call for a large vessel to be filled with a mixture of all the liquors stocked in the bar. Such an alcoholic compound was free to all passengers while it lasted. It was traditionally drunk from glasses modelled vaguely on the body of a cockerel, with a stirring-rod resembling its tail. So they called this type of drink cocktails. Unlike your other legends, I have seen some visual proof for this notion. It was an illustration to the words of a long-forgotten ballad, entitled 'An American Cock-tale' – t-a-l-e." John B. spelt it out. "Roughly portrayed in the picture are a glass and rod something like the style I mentioned. Albeit that this sheet was published in 1871, that doesn't debar the word cocktail from being of much earlier usage: we know it was. But it could indeed have been first used on those steamers."

"I'm afraid not, John," said Al, who is something of an historian. "Cocktail had been defined as a type of drink before there were any Mississippi steamers."

We discussed this point, and got nowhere.

* * *

"I read somewhere," said James, turning towards me, "a theory attributed to you that Dr. Samuel Johnson applied the word cocktail to a drink made with gin and vermouth. Palpably absurd for any manner of reasons."

"Of course, and meant to be. In a book on the Dry Martini, I interpolated an imaginary excerpt from an unknown bit of Boswell's biography of Johnson. But in that fanciful interlude I did indicate what I firmly believe is the most likely origin of cocktail."

David Jermyn was dozing: my other friends showed more interest. I told them:

"In the eighteenth and early nineteenth centuries, it was the custom to dock – or cock – the tail of a horse of good breeding yet not a true thoroughbred. Such an animal was known as cock-tailed or a cocktail. The horsey fraternity, in Britain and the United States, were hard-drinking and much addicted to strong spiced cups and punches. So it would be wholly logical if they transferred the name for a horse of mixed provenance to a drink of mixed ingredients."

On the theories put forward, there was no unanimous conclusion, though the equine derivation was by a majority considered the most plausible, with *Coquetel* next.

We arranged to meet shortly to discuss cocktails in their modern application.

AFTER THAT FROLIC, SOME FACTS ON COCKTAILS' PROGRESS ARE IN ORDER.

It is generally conceded that the first cocktail book at all seriously to impinge on public consciousness was the one compiled by Jerry Thomas. His _Bon Vivant's Guide, or How To Mix Drinks_ came out in 1862. He had previously toured Europe, researching his subject: I do not see why, since his own country was far in advance in this field. He had £1000 of solid silver bar equipment with him, which helped engender publicity, and that may have been what the trip was about. He had a definite, if very muted, effect on conservative European drinking patterns. Jerry was a Californian, and in California he invented the sickly Martinez cocktail – cause of later confusion: see chapter 8 (Classic of Classics). Jerry became a celebrity at the Metropolitan Hotel, New York City.

Also claiming to have studied in Europe was Jerry's fellow-countryman and Californian, Harry Johnson, whom I think deserves more attention than he has received in the bibliography of drinks and drinking. In 1869 he won the championship of the United States in what may be claimed as the first

important cocktail contest. Although there were only five other challengers, they were, said Johnson, "five of the most popular and scientific bartenders of the day." We do not know if Jerry Thomas was one of them. The tourney (Harry's word) took place in New Orleans. A year earlier, Harry had sunk his savings in a bar in Chicago, described with his usual modesty as "recognised as the finest establishment of its kind in the country".

Before leaving his native state for good, in San Francisco Harry had issued "the first *Bartender's Manual* ever in the United States." He said he sold 10,000 copies. None appears to have survived: did it antedate *The Bon Vivant's Guide?*

Harry lost his all in the great Chicago fire of 1871. He obtained employment in Boston before settling in New York, where he was eventually able to "begin in business of my own, which has since been pre-eminently successful."

In 1882, Harry Johnson, describing himself as "Publisher and Professional Bartender and Instructor of the Art of How to Attend a Bar", put out, from his address in Hanover Square, New York City, a book called *The New and Improved Bartender's Manual, or How to Mix Drinks in the Present Style.* I feel his sub-title was having a knock at Thomas's work of twenty years earlier. It cost one dollar, a fairly hefty price when you consider that he recorded paying his staff under 2 dollars a day plus 40 cents for their meals. We would more or less easily recognise Harry's Gin Sling, Gin Sour, or Gin Fizz, but, amongst his many other gin mixes, I doubt if we would fancy his Gin and Wormwood or Gin and Molasses.

* * *

Neither of those pioneers, Thomas and Johnson, worked in a period when dry gin was the style for mixed drinks: if they knew unsweetened gin, they had not time for it. Yet cocktail drinking was already part of daily upper class life in the United States. It took another big step forward when, in 1892, Heublein's, of Hartford, Connecticut, introduced bottled proprietary cocktails. Their very first was a gin mix, a Martini (probably sweetened gin and Martini red vermouth plus minor items), which had little connection with the Dry Martini cocktail to come. Cocktails had been bottled for some time – as a home activity – and they were thus particularly used for sporting parties and similar alfresco events. The Heublein range was soon extended and it allowed hostesses to serve cocktails without danger of making mistakes in their preparation. Advertising for bottled cocktails was distinctly up-market and quite often aimed at women.

However, they ordered things differently in Britain. There, at the turn of the century, cocktails had some way to go to attain the status they enjoyed across the Atlantic. This was well illustrated by John Galsworthy in *The Forsyte Saga*: wishing to emphasise the caddishness of Montague Dartie, profligate spender of his Forsyte-wife's money, he pictured him drinking a cocktail whilst Queen Victoria's funeral cortege (1901) passed his club.

Britain waited until after World War I truly to adopt the cocktail habit.

NOTES

FABLES, MYTHS AND LEGENDS

The imaginary conversations embrace such stories as have come into my ken on this subject. Does it the least matter why cocktail came to have the meaning it does? No – but it is fun: cocktails are fun. What is life without an element of fantasy?

The book in which I am quoted regarding Dr. Johnson is Tony Lord's very comprehensive *The World Guide to Spirits*. Tony cannot seriously have been taken in by my obvious spoof attribution of the origin of cocktail (in drinking terms) to the great lexicographer: but that is how "instant history" is created!

The Betsy Flanagan tale was given renewed circulation by Harold J. Grossman in his celebrated *Grossman's Guide*. Versions of this story exist which do not involve Yankies but transpose the setting to the Deep South with even less credibility.

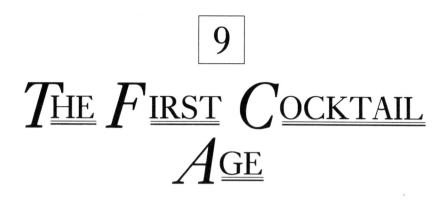

9

THE FIRST COCKTAIL AGE

1930 EFFECTS OF PROHIBITION

Letter from Hubert B. Schuyler II, of New York City, to a friend in London, of whom we only know the forename but whom we may assume was in the gin trade or, at least, a devoted drinker of gin.

Dear Jack,

You have asked me to comment on certain specific aspects of the Great American Drought which has now beset our country for a decade. You are correct in suggesting that gin has been one of the beneficiaries of national Prohibition, which has given such impetus to cocktail drinking that some are referring to the Cocktail Age, just as they called the 'twenties the Jazz Age. The two go well together.

Regretfully, one must in candour say that some of gin's popularity is because it is the simplest of spirits to produce at all satisfactorily at home – what we call 'bath-tub gin'. Much of it is ghastly stuff, but, with reasonable care, it won't kill. If one can get some decent neutral alcohol from an obliging pharmacist – the most reliable source – by following instructions that are readily obtainable, one can make a passable substitute for real gin. It will make a tolerable cocktail if the ingredients are flavoursome enough. I need hardly say I would not drink such 'gin' – even in a cocktail – and I recognise I am privileged. Friends of mine, worse hit by the Wall Street disaster last year, have been reduced to 'bath-tub gin'.

Because of the expense, or through inability to find proper spirit, some folk have taken to distilling their own alcohol. At best, this is very raw, full of unpleasant, often dangerous, elements. Then there is the terrible 'hooch' peddled by slippery ruffians whom I would not dignify by the term

bootlegger. This illicit liquor is frequently industrial alcohol, just about drinkable, liable to cause nauseous intoxication and leading to blindness, insanity and death. I would think it better the federal authorities proceeded against the criminals who deal in such poisons rather than prosecuting comparatively honest citizens who provide real, if illegal, liquor for respectable folk. "Moonshining" (I think you'll recognise the word), which is a cherished American tradition, is practised on an industrial scale. It diverts effort by government officers – G-Men is the slang phrase for them – which might be better directed elsewhere.

Though the expense is considerable, I have no difficulty in obtaining the London gin for which we share a preference since my personal stock ran out a couple of years ago. We call untampered imported spirit "the real McCoy", I rarely go to speakeasies: my club is well supplied with liquor which, in theory at least, was purchased before 1920. The police don't bother us, and it is not for me to ask why! In advance of my cellar's total depletion, I had made discreet enquiries. Now I enjoy regular deliveries to the door of my apartment. A polite young man – not always the same one – hands a large plain package to my butler, with the words "Mr. Schuyler's special order". My man hands over a previously agreed amount of dollars: I am not concerned with details, and I have little doubt that a commission is involved. I do not know, or wish to meet, my bootlegger: sufficient to me that I get genuine gin. Wine I still have in sufficient quantity for two or three years. I cannot see myself as a lawbreaker. It is not an offence to possess liquor for personal use and my part in illegal trading is too trivial to give me any qualms.

Now, as to this Cocktail Age. It is nothing new so far as the wealthier classes are concerned: the revolution lies in the spread of the cocktail habit to sections of society to whom it is a novelty. In the circles in which I move, even in my youth it was customary to serve a Martini, a Bronx or one of the better-known cocktails before meals, whether or not we were entertaining. My father considered gin the only proper base for mixed drinks: I seem to have inherited that preference, though my taste in cocktails is more catholic than his. Formerly, outside the cosmopolitan cities, spirits were not much drunk – if one excepts frontier saloons. In metropolitan centres, the spirit of the mass population was whiskey – and I don't mean fine Bourbon. Gin was, at one end of the scale, a lower class liquor: at the other, it was drunk in cocktails by the upper crust (if you will pardon the phrase).

These drinking patterns changed dramatically when the Drys triumphed. Deny people something, and they will instantly want it. So large tracts of our country that scarcely knew spirits became thirsty for them. People who would not otherwise have done so, acquired a taste for strong liquor. But the liquor available was mostly of a very poor kind: with the natural inventiveness of Americans, they evolved a proliferation of hitherto unknown mixes. Fruit juices, cordials, medicinal bitters, synthetic flavourings – anything to hide the awfulness of the spirit whilst retaining its kick. Fancy names were given to these concoctions – new ones arrive every day – and the odd thing is that folk who had access to perfectly good liquor started to ape the absurdities of their less fortunate compatriots. There are perfectly respectable friends of mine who are making ridiculous concoctions – are proud of their ingenuity. They do not even let their servants mix these drinks but themselves act as bartenders! I don't think of myself as fuddy-duddy, yet I do deplore waste of costly liquor. The hoi-polloi, the common drunkard, the dowager, the banker – all are drinking weird mixes. Yes, it is indeed the Cocktail Age.

However, I see some good emerging from the bad. In the long run, "bath-tub gin" has done no harm to the real product: it has become a jokey, almost affectionate description, rather as "mother's ruin" has with you. It may have helped gin gain new devotees. Numerous people of my acquaintance, who did not use gin much before Prohibition because they have acquired the cocktail habit, now demand good gin from their suppliers.

I do not think repeal of the 18th amendment to the Constitution can be far away. The Wets steadily gain ground. This year, the American Bar Association overwhelmingly voted in favour of repeal. The influential Association Against the Prohibition Amendment, which I strongly support, gains strength by the month. Its treasurer, Charles Sabin, has a wife who is a leader of Society in this city, and she has enlisted as allies such persons as Mrs. Pierre Dupont, Mrs. August Belmont, Mrs. Archibald Roosevelt and Mrs. Coffin Van Raennselaer. These names may not mean much to you, but I assure you they carry considerable weight in political quarters.

When repeal comes, as it must do, liquor will flow legally into this country. Those who have had to have resource to "hooch" gins will move to the real product, if they can afford to. American distillers, where they have not gone bankrupt, and enterprising overseas companies, will start distilling on a scale hitherto unknown – all because of a demand created by the Dry scourge. Myself, I look forward to the day when I can have my merchant openly deliver: my butler will have to do without his cut! Despite depressed financial conditions here, I have booked on the Mauretania and should be drinking a Dry Martini with my English friends within a few weeks.

THE BRITISH SCENE

By 1930, the Cocktail Age was in full swing in the United Kingdom. However, it took a very different form to that of the U.S.A. It was nothing like so widespread. Cocktails were confined to the Bright Young Things, to a tiny sophisticated section of the population, who made up Society. But these people were much written about: the Cocktail Age was vicariously enjoyed by millions who never saw a cocktail, let alone drank one. Well-thumbed copies of the *Tatler* and many other glossy magazines, in hairdressers' and dentists' waiting-rooms (the funeral parlours of journals), brought the glamour of cocktail parties into drab lives. Old aristocratic society deplored the excesses of the "cocktail set": the submerged unemployed scarcely knew it existed. Britain's Cocktail Age was highly London-orientated: it was peopled by the upper middle-class, by the New Rich, by the "smart" artistic cliques, by style-setting celebrities and would-be celebrities: above all, by the affluent young. The demographic scope of this Cocktail Age was infinitely narrower than the American one. And yet its influence was big. It enormously improved gin's image.

In the 'thirties in Britain, a bottle of gin cost approximately one-quarter of an unskilled workingman's weekly wage. Despite this, a great deal of gin was drunk in public houses. Remember the fillip it received from the eclipse of grain whisky. At least it was all good gin: Britons enjoyed jokes about Prohibition, which King George V had dubbed "an outrage." Old Tom gin still had its increasingly ageing adherents, there was some demand for Dutch gin, and flavoured gins (mainly orange and lemon) were popular: however, gin, without prefix, now meant London dry gin. As a style of gin it was a clear leader in a field it was soon totally to dominate. In pubs, broadly speaking the preferred mixers were (in roughly ascending order of prestige) – peppermint, orange squash, ginger beer, sweet vermouth, tonic-water, Dubonnet, dry vermouth. Pink Gin (q.v.) was more a home drink or for the cocktail bars and cocktail lounges of big cities. The ordinary pub, even smartish ones, did not serve cocktails at all: only a few even had ice! Right into modern times, many an American tourist has unwarily asked for a 'Martini' in a pub and been alarmed to be served with a glass of warm red vermouth.

The Cocktail Age drooped, so far as Britain is concerned, around 1937. Perhaps due to its flippancy, the cocktail habit lost some of its aura as it became fashionable to espouse Causes as the skies darkened over Europe. For home hospitality, the cocktail party tended to be replaced by the rather boring sherry party. The gin-and-tonic ousted more outrageous mixes. In a nutshell, cocktails were by no means extinguished but veered towards the more traditional and sensible – and then became dormant during the war years, both through the seriousness of the times and because liquor was severely restricted.

NOTES

1930 EFFECTS OF PROHIBITION

Mr. Schuyler was a snob: that is obvious. His letter is a device to record some opinions on the influence of Prohibition on drinking patterns, particularly in relation to gin. His anti-Prohibition body existed.

"The real McCoy", one of several of Prohibition's linguistic contributions, came from Captain Bill McCoy, who operated from the Bahamas. As a bootlegger, the Captain gained such a reputation for unvarying quality and lack of skullduggery, that when his rivals wished to impress a customer they would claim that what they were offering was "the real McCoy" – which, of course, was not always true. McCoy retired, with a million dollars, before Repeal.

As our Hubert Schuyler forecast, Prohibition was ended in 1933 and after Repeal the demand for gin was vastly greater than it had been in 1920. The Schuylers of this world could have their imported London gin, but the Depression was deep and most Americans drank domestic gin (including "moonshine", which continued to flourish). As soon as practicable, Gordon's started production in the U.S.A., with immense success.

THIS SEEMS THE POINT AT WHICH TO INTRODUCE THE FIRST OF TWO SHORT LISTS OF GIN DRINKS (NOT ALL COCKTAILS)

The following selection is complementary to the "classics" detailed in chapter 7. I add informative notes where applicable: an unbroken compilation of recipes is boring. I see no point to recapitulating ephemeral frivolities from the Cocktail Age. I estimate there are in print at least ten thousand cocktail recipes, about a third of them involving gin. Of these, perhaps two hundred are worth consideration, and half that number worth making. Some do repay attention handsomely. A few are amusing curiosities.

NOTE

Numerals in a recipe refer to a measure/jigger of 1 fluid ounce or about 25 ml if you must go metric. (The British and American ounces are not identical but so close as to make no practical difference.)

With an intelligent readership, I do not think it needful to give detailed instructions about suitable glasses after "shake" or "mix" or "strain", nor to say "with ice" repeatedly, unless a particular sort of ice is recommended. I take it everyone knows what is meant by "on-the-rocks". Garnish is for individual preference.

There are few rules in mixing drinks, but one is that you cannot make first-class drinks except with first class ingredients.

A recipe is not immutable law: it is a guideline for the uninitiated and a recommendation for the informed.

GIN DRINKS 1.

Most of these drinks pre-date the Cocktail Age or were evolved and gained popularity during that period, say 1920–39.

ALEXANDER

1 dry gin
1 crème de cacao
2 fresh cream

Shake vigorously and strain. Sprinkle touch of nutmeg on top.

Today the Brandy Alexander is the best-known, but the gin version is older. There are numerous Alexander recipes, going back a century.

BACCIO PUNCH

1 standard bottle dry gin
1 pint (575 ml) unsweetened grapefruit juice
1 bottle non-vintage champagne (or superior dry sparkling wine)
1½ pints (say a siphon) soda-water
half-bottle of liqueur (see below)

Mix ingredients, other than sparkling wine, in large bowl with plenty of ice. Add fruits in season as available and at own discretion. At last moment, add wine (well chilled).
Note: the liqueur called for in original recipe is anisette. If you dislike that as much as I do, substitute Cointreau or Grand Marnier.

This is not an inexpensive party drink: it may give you ideas for your own cold punch.

BRONX

2 dry gin
½ dry vermouth
½ dry red vermouth
1 fresh orange juice

Shake and strain. Cherry decoration usual.

This enduring cocktail was probably invented early this century at the Waldorf Hotel, New York City, and named after the Bronx Zoo.

BUNNY HUG

1 dry gin
1 Pernod
1 whiskey

Shake and strain.

Personally, I think this is about as nasty a cocktail as I know of. I include it because it has, for some reason, become a pseudo-classic. One assumes it was invented to disguise 'hooch'.

CLOVER CLUB

2 dry gin
2 lemon juice
1 grenadine syrup
white of an egg

Shake vigorously and strain. Sometimes topped with soda-water but best undiluted.

This deservedly classic, but somewhat neglected, mix belongs to the Collins/Sling/Fizz category: to my mind, the best of them all.

COLLINS

See chapter 7 (1834) and Notes.

DOG'S NOSE

2 dry gin (or more)
1 glass draught beer

This is here for historical reasons. The mix was popular in Victorian England – a quick intoxicant – but mercifully vanished, or I hope so. If stout was the beer, nutmeg was usually dusted on top.

DRY MARTINI

See chapter 7 (1912) and Notes. Also Martini (below)

FIBBER McGEE

2 dry gin
1 fresh grapefruit juice
1 rosso vermouth
3 dashes Angostura

Shake and strain.

GIBSON

See chapter 7 (1928).

GIMLET

See chapter 7 (1857).

GIN COBBLER

Dissolve teaspoon caster sugar in a little water in tall glass.
Half fill with crushed ice. Add
2 dry gin
teaspoon lemon or fresh lime juice

Stir. Garnish with fruit to personal taste. Top with soda-water. Serve with straws.

GIN COCKTAIL

2 dry gin
3 dashes orange bitters

Stir and strain. Add zest of orange peel.

This is perhaps the simplest of all cocktails; in fact, some might say it doesn't fill the criteria for being called a cocktail.

GIN CRUSTA

Frost rim of wine glass by moistening with lemon juice and dipping in fine sugar. Place long spiral of lemon peel in the glass. Separately –

2 dry gin
½ lemon juice
½ Cointreau
teaspoon maraschino
dash of Angostura

Shake, and strain into prepared glass.

GIN FIZZ

See chapter 8 (1834) and Notes.

GIN-GIN

2 dry gin
2 ginger wine

May be lightly iced, but best not – in winter anyway.

There is a town called Gin-Gin in Australia: (dept. of Useless Information).

GIN & GINGER (1)

2 dry gin
ginger ale
slice of lemon/lime

Mix with ice in tall glass, using American ginger ale, or Schweppes Original for less sweetness.

GIN & GINGER (2)

2 dry gin
ginger beer
slice of lemon/lime

Mix with ice in tall glass. This is the more traditional of the two. Unfortunately ginger beer is not now universally available: what is, is sweeter than old-time "stone ginger" and extra lemon juice is advised. A very refreshing drink.

GIN JULEP

In a large tumbler, crush 3 sprigs of fresh mint, together with level teaspoon caster sugar.
Almost fill glass with crushed ice.
Stir, and add at least
2 dry gin

Decorate with sprig of mint.

Julep has become so associated with the Mint Julep made with Bourbon that it is forgotten that Julep once covered a variety of drinks. Over a century ago, a Gin Julep was listed in a recipe book: it was made with 'Holland' gin. Julep, as a drink, is of considerable antiquity. Samuel Pepys records enjoying "a can of good julep", but we don't know its constituents. Julep (from the Arabic julab – rose water) also came to describe any pleasing concoction to make evil-flavoured medicines more palatable.

GIN & LEMON

This can mean gin with lemon squash or with the fizzy lemonade so popular in Britain (or 7-Up). Gin goes well with any mixers – cola for example – so that it is superfluous to mention all possible combinations.

GIN & ORANGE

With chilled fresh orange juice, this is a marvellous cooler. With orange squash it is a long-time favourite in British pubs. What proportions you use, how much ice and so on are purely for personal decision.

GIN RICKEY

See chapter 7 (1890) and Notes.

Though it is sometimes said a Rickey may be made with any spirit, the original gin version is indubitably the best.

GIN SIN

2 dry gin
½ orange juice
½ lemon juice
teaspoon grenadine syrup

Shake and strain.

GIN SLING

See chapter 7 (1834) and Notes; also Singapore Gin Sling.

GIN SOUR

1½ dry gin
1 meon juice
half-teaspoon caster sugar

Shake and strain. Add slice of lemon and optionally.

GIN TWIST

This is an archaic term (early 18th century slang) and is included for its historical associations, though I can find no recipes for it, nor descriptions, in cocktail-books ancient or modern. It appears that a Twist – a Gin Twist is the most frequently mentioned in literature – was any liqour mixed with one other ingredient, such as the once popular gin-and-peppermint. But it could also be applied to a mix of two non-alcoholic beverages.

HIGHBALL

Effectively, any simple long spirituous drink. The name comes from the early days of American railroads. A ball on a pole was used to signal to locomen: if raised high, it indicated he was behind schedule and should put on steam. So it became applied to a drink that could be quickly prepared for speedy consumption.

See Bulldog Highball (chapter 10).

GIN & TONIC

See chapter 7 (1865) and Notes.

HOBSON

2 sloe gin
1 Cointreau
½ Pernod

Shake and strain.

This was named after a hero of the American-Spanish War of 1898 who became a well-known Congressman. He was an ardent abstainer, so this mix was definitely not "Hobson's Choice".

HORSE'S NECK

Hang a spiral of lemon peel inside a tall glass and quarter-fill it with ice.
2 dry gin
dash of Angostura

Top with ginger ale.

MARTINEZ

1½ dry gin
½ red vermouth
teaspoon maraschino
dash of orange bitters

Stir and strain.

This is one simplified version, of many, founded on Jerry Thomas's recipe. He was said to have invented it for a customer, in his San Francisco bar, who was suffering from a hangover (which this mix would have seriously worsened). However, the stranger was deeply impressed by the drink, for which Jerry yet had no name. All Jerry could recall of the appreciative man was that he said he was travelling to Martinez township. The original Martinez cocktail was complicated, made with Old Tom gin and decidedly sweet. There is no connection with the Dry Martini.

MARTINI

See chapter 7 (1912) and Notes.

In a smart bar situation, the Dry Martini is often simply "a Martini"; viz. "A Martini, very dry, straight-up".

MARTINI (MEDIUM)

2 dry gin
teaspoon (or less) each of red and dry vermouth.

Stir and strain. Optionally, add zest of lemon peel.

MARTINI (SWEET)

2 dry gin
1 red vermouth

Stir and strain. Optionally, add small slice of lemon.

NEGRONI

1½ dry gin
1½ red vermouth
1 Campari

Serve on-the-rocks. Top with soda-water. Add slice of orange.

PERFECT

This is the same as Trinity (q.v.), though some pundits add a dash of Angostura. That notable cocktailman, David Embury, says Perfect is a misnomer. Ideal is another name under which the same recipe appears, but I give quite a different version (chapter 10). The titles of cocktails can be extremely confusing: I have seen a Bronx listed as made with Canadian whisky!

PINK GIN

See chapter 8 (1826) and Notes.

PINK LADY

2 dry gin
2 cream
1 grenadine syrup
½ lemon juice

Shake briskly and strain.

There are various cocktails similar to this. Stan Jones says it became formalised as above in 1912 and named for the play "Pink Lady" presented on Broadway that year. This is a fairly early example of a cream cocktail. Such creamy mixes have become very popular in modern times: they tend to be bland and sweet.

RAMOS FIZZ

2 dry gin
1 lemon or fresh lime juice
teaspoon each of kirsch and caster sugar
half white of an egg

Shake briskly and strain on-the-rocks in tall glass. Serve with straws.

I have slightly adapted this recipe from the original which called for orange-flower water, a commodity not likely to be handy today. My version follows that of British expert Eddie Clarke.

Also known as New Orleans Fizz, this was a speciality of Henrico Ramos, of that city, who owned the Imperial Cabinet Saloon in the 1880s. This place was so popular that, during Mardi Gras, Ramos employed thirty boys just to shake drinks.

RICKEY

See Gin Rickey

ROLLS ROYCE

2 dry gin
1 red vermouth
½ Bénédictine
½ dry vermouth

Shake and strain.

SIDECAR

See chapter 11.

SILVER STREAK (1)

1½ dry gin
1½ kümmel

Pour over finely crushed ice in small wine-glass. Serve with straws.

SILVER STREAK (2)

1½ dry gin
1½ kümmel
teaspoon lemon juice

Shake and strain.

These Silver Streaks might be described as digestive rather than aperitif cocktails.

SINGAPORE GIN SLING

2 dry gin
2 fresh lime (lemon) juice
2 level teaspoons caster sugar

Pour on to crushed ice in tall glass. Top with soda-water. Pour on top.

½ Cointreau
½ Peter Heering cherry liqueur

Stir briefly. Garnish with round of lime (lemon). Serve with straws.

This famous drink is more celebrated in reputation than through consumption today. It is said to have been first mixed in the Raffles Hotel, Singapore, during World War I: I believe it to date from earlier. So does Stan (Complete Barguide) Jones who thinks it derives from the Straits Sling: he gives a recipe from early this century. He also lists a version from the 1930s. Both contain Bénédictine and vary considerably from my (correct?) recipe. A picture from a modern Raffles Hotel publicity card, sent me by Mrs. Maria Garford, illustrates a Singapore Gin Sling as having a creamy head and desecrated by fruit and other "garbage", mot juste of David Embury for sundry additions to drinks by way of superfluous decorative junk. This is an example of how classic recipes become mutated from their original straightforwardness.

TRINITY

1 dry gin
1 red vermouth
1 dry vermouth

Shake and strain.

This is a grander version of what was once called Gin-and-Mixed, for which the ingredients were simply poured into a glass, usually without ice.

WHITE LADY

See chapter 7 (1925) and Notes.

* * *

"There is no such thing as *one* Dry Martini."
John Bradley Hutton.

* * *

"One Dry Martini is necessary; two are dangerous; three are not enough."

10

GIN TODAY

Before we come to our own times, a glance at the 1939–46 period is necessary to complete gin's human history.

THE WAR YEARS

The Second World War meant curtains for a Cocktail Age that was, in any event, declining. In certain neutral cases, or countries distanced from battle zones, drinking patterns were comparatively unaffected. For many millions, social life was dislocated, or simply vanished. Not that people stopped drinking: even in prisoner-of-war camps some sorts of distillates were produced.

In the United States, conditions were less irksome than in Britain, whence ships, sailing perilously to collect munitions, carried cargoes of gin and whisky, of which the British market was starved. In the U.S.A., many distillers turned to making industrial alcohol for the war effort. Even before Pearl Harbour, Lewis Rosensteil, head of Schenley's, with patriotic foresight adapted some of his facilities to that purpose: when his chemists invented a way to speed distillation of commercial alcohol, he allowed his rivals free access to it.

In Britain, spirits were placed on a quota basis – a small fraction of pre-war sales was allowed to the wholesale and retail trades. A consumer's gin "allowance" – it was never officially rationed – was reckoned to work out at about a bottle a month, if he ever saw it. Like all things in short supply, gin went "under the counter": a black market speedily grew up, which was not technically illegal. What was illegal were concoctions labelled "gin" that were peddled to the unwary or greedy by the "spiv" sub-culture that battened on shortages. John Watney quotes, as an example, "Edgware Road gin", so called because it was believed to be made in the area of that London thoroughfare: some maintained it was made *from* it, for it tasted strongly of tar. Such spirits were at best adulterated real gin: at worst they were diluted and clumsily flavoured industrial methanol, actively poisonous and, if not lethal as was often the case, carrying hideous side-effects. A situation arose that was a microcosm of Prohibition. The equivalent of bootleggers distributed dubiously obtained real gin, or doctored real gin, and villains dealt in noxious hooch. Matters were not helped by the bombing in early blitzes, but not the total destruction, of London's two biggest distilleries. An eye-witness to one of these disasters told me he saw gin flowing down the gutters in a torrent which some amateur firemen found it impossible to resist, so that their attention to the gin-fuelled conflagration was diminished. At the same establishment, an incendiary bomb fell into a huge vat of gin, which extinguished it: my informant could not recall, or was reluctant to tell me, what happened to the precious spirit. Bombs obliterated the famous old distillery in Plymouth (q.v.). The London distilleries just managed to keep up production by heroic improvisation and without loss of quality.

Shortly after the outbreak of war, excise taxes on spirits had been doubled. This did not effect the big cities where there was more money than things on which to spend it, which accounted for black market prosperity. But there were curious results elsewhere, as I found out. For a time, I was secretary to a large headquarters officers' mess in a requisitioned hotel in the Yorkshire countryside. I had a very enterprising mess sergeant and, after I had taken over a bar which had been relying on exiguous Army supplies of spirits, he explained things to me. There was many a remote public house, formerly doing good business, which found itself, through mobilisation and drafting into factories, virtually without customers except for a few old-timers and agricultural workers who had neither the taste nor means for spirits. These places had quotas based on sales they could no longer make. Yet they wished to retain their quotas against an eventual up-turn and were happy to sell most of their spirits at cost to maintain a cash-flow. They were too ingenuous or honest, these bucolic landlords, to realise they could get twice their costs in a town, and at this stage of the war the spivs had not yet got at them: I expect things changed later. Anyway, I would get hold of a staff car on some pretext, give my sergeant a substantial sum of money, and off he would go into the wilds with instructions not to come back until he was out of funds. No mess in the region had a bar like ours: visiting officers were astounded and my fellow officers most appreciative. The mess president, a "dug out" major, asked no awkward questions. I did nothing illegal in law, though I dare say I bent a few King's Regulations. I was sorry when I was posted away, for never again for the duration did I have such easy access to gin: I was often reduced to drinking beer, and pretty awful most wartime beer was.

Even when one got real gin, one's problems were not entirely conquered, unless one liked gin and water, a taste which I had yet to acquire (and which is now my preferred daily tipple). Decent cocktails were out of the question after supplies of vermouth and liqueurs ran out: there were some rather beastly substitutes. Citrus fruits were virtually unknown. There was concentrated orange juice for children, and quite a lot of this found its way into mixed drinks, though it was not all that satisfactory. You could not have a proper gin-and-tonic: all mixers and similar products were nationalised under SDI (Soft Drinks Industries) and were of uniform insipidity. For a glorious spell, when I was attached to Supreme Allied H.Q. (SHAEF) in London, I enjoyed a quota of gin from the PX, but that privilege was speedily withdrawn as Britons on the staff grew in numbers. I did know a few bartenders who kept the real stuff for pre-war regulars – but generally speaking those were hard days for gin-drinkers, or any drinkers.

* * *

The coming of peace did not instantly bring relief. Gin remained on quota, though it was eased earlier than in the case of whisky. Comparatively soon after the war, bars had almost adequate supplies, though in 1947 in London I still had to pay double the proper retail price to ensure getting as much as I wanted of my preferred brand. Whisky continued in short supply well after gin was freely available, and, when it became unrestricted, gin sales boomed: for the first time, a London distillery hit the million cases a year mark – to be greatly exceeded not long afterwards.

GIN'S BATTLES

Emergence of normality in the trade found gin in an improved position. Dry gin was indisputably the totally dominant style. The number of brands was fewer than it had been, and was further to decrease. Cocktails had virtually vanished, except in a tiny social stratum: the diplomatic cocktail party was about the only residual manifestation of that genre of entertainment. In Britain, austerity was the order of the day: food rationing continued officially until 1953! With the demise of SDI (see above), decent tonic-water was again to be had: gin-and-tonic was the smart thing to drink. In business circles, cocktails were used, but in a conservative way: in top bars, the range of cocktails was traditional. The Dry Martini re-asserted its supremacy as a mix, now proper dry vermouth was back. But cocktails meant even less to the broad mass of the public than they had in the 'thirties. Gin they drank aplenty – as gin-and-orange, gin-and-It (red vermouth), or other simple mixes. The United Kingdom Bartenders' Guild made efforts to promote cocktails by means of competitions: they engendered some publicity but left the ordinary gin-drinker unmoved. In the United States, where things move faster, cocktails were right back in fashion: the ultra-dry Martini was becoming the thing. Gin reigned supreme: it had no real rivals amongst white spirits. However, there was a pale cloud on its horizon.

That cloud was, of course, vodka. It was not any part of this book's function to outline or explain the extraordinary rise of the totally featureless distillate the West knows as vodka, but it must be mentioned for its impingement on gin. From the mid-'forties, the growth in popularity of vodka – by association a Russian product and thus fitting oddly into the American scene – was sensational in the U.S.A. This happened at a time when spirit sales were buoyant, but its affect on gin was nonetheless formidable. Yet it is a further tribute to gin's resilience, its enduring hold on drinkers' affections, that gin did not succumb to this powerful product competition. In the United States in particular, gin has not only had to combat the vogue for vodka, but those for white rum and, latterly, for tequila, the peculiar Mexican *aguardiente*. Gin has had to fight before – against foolish laws, against disrepute, against other products, against official repression, against shortage, against Prohibition – and has won every time. To have survived, let alone to have prospered, gin must have something very special about it – such as character, salubrity, adaptability.

When the fashion for vodka and white rum crossed the Atlantic – tequila has barely taken off in Britain – the impact was less immediate than in the U.S.A. It is rather a question of by how much more consumption of gin would have risen without that competition. The inference I draw is that the young, rebellious against the preferences of their elders, make a market for new spirits – and for mixes, too. As they mature, a high proportion of them turn to more established products: in white spirit, that means gin. With maturity comes discretion and knowledge; for most people anyway. Yet it must be faced that gin took some hard knocks in the 'sixties and 'seventies. Was gin getting a slightly fuddy-duddy image? Did the young think it rather old-hat? A fresh phenomenon came to revivify gin's fortunes.

A NEW COCKTAIL AGE

I take modest pride that in 1966 I forecast a return to cocktail-drinking, when the habit was still confined to a minute minority of the British population: it was infinitely more widespread in the United States. Foreign travel must have influenced a much more catholic approach to drinks in notoriously unprogressive Britons; a wider spread of money, less parental direction, these may have encouraged a more enterprising attitude in home entertaining and to drinking in bars. One can only submit the broadest notions as to why cocktails have spread to all segments of the community, so that nowadays the word is as well understood in workingmen's clubs, raucous discotheques, in many a pub, as it is in the Ritz or snaziest niterie.

That is what so distinguishes today's cocktail cult from its forerunner: the fashion for cocktails is confined to no particular financial or social classification: it is democratic in the best sense, and also very much unisex. Whereas cocktails were once exclusive, they are now inclusive. The extremely expensive new cocktail-bar-cum-restaurants of London's West End serve basically the same drinks as a disco in Wigan.

The new fashion for cocktails has its quirks, just like the first – but quite different ones. Though there are again some odd, and transient, mixes around, elaboration of mixes is less to be seen in strange and incompatible ingredients than in esoteric decoration. Many cocktails have become visually as bizarre as their forerunners were eccentric in content. Often a sensible blend of gin and harmonious ingredients is served in a fantastical glass, enhanced (if that be the correct word) with exotic stirring rod, multi-hued misshapen straws, plastic animals and a jumble of impaled fruit, plus ghastly miniature parasol. A whole industry has grown up to supply such embellishments which, I suspect, are sometimes employed to camouflage fairly trite recipes. I do not condemn: I record – although I am founder, and so far sole member, of OPTIC (Organisation for Prevention of Thingamajigs in Cocktails)!

This vogue for cocktails is to be praised. It is delightful that more adventuresomeness is being shown by young drinkers everywhere: it does not the least put off the solid core of regular gin-drinkers who happen to prefer gin and are uninfluenced by fashion – for cocktails or anything else – that they consider as passing whims, which I do not think cocktails are this time round. It is socially admirable that a young man who might previously have gone to a pub to get drunk with his male friends now takes his girl there to share a civilised and amusing drink. From a British viewpoint, it is a major revolution that an ordinary pub should serve cocktails at all: an increasing number make and (profitably) sell them. Pre-mixes are often used, which have never caught on for home mixing as they have in American households. Many of these modern cocktails are not particularly alcoholic: the long, diluted and sweet tends to oust the short and strong.

The move towards weaker cocktails started in the U.S.A., home of virtually every drinking fashion. The decline of the Dry Martini has been mentioned already. Latterly, there have been recipes specially designed to use smaller than usual amounts of alcohol, and low-strength versions of traditional spirits have been introduced, which (as I write) must be labelled "diluted" so as not to deceive purchasers (see chapter 12 – Sub-Normal).

I risk another forecast. Cocktails are here to stay. But the grotesque aspects of modern mixes will not. Today's drinkers of dolled-up, mutton-dressed-as-lamb cocktails will be tomorrow's customers for simpler, or traditional, recipes – and a majority of those are gin-based. Get in touch with me in ten years!

WHAT *IS* A COCKTAIL?

Because of the peculiarly close connection between gin and cocktails, I am pursuing another aspect of the topic. We have dealt with the notions of *why* a cocktail may be so called: now for the *what*. I have frequently been asked the question. Cocktail is now used to cover drinks formerly classified as crustas, fixes, cups, punches, sours, smashes, cobblers, daisies, sangarees, flips, and other categoric names.

Strangely, not in Britain – nor, I think, anywhere else – has what constitutes a cocktail been legally established. This is potentially more important than it may seem. In the United Kingdom, where spirits are retailed by the tot, a measure must be used which is in content not less than one-sixth of a gill (approx. 2.5 cls) for serving gin, whisky, vodka or rum (brandy was overlooked when the regulation was made). The size of an establishment's basic measure must be displayed. (A gill is a quarter-pint, the old quartern – once the standard measure for a tot of gin in more spacious days.)

It is accepted that for a cocktail these minimum measures do not apply. So we come to the point: what *is* a cocktail? The generally held opinion is that a cocktail has at least three ingredients. But is ice an ingredient? Is a twist of peel? Is a dash of Angostura? Is water? For if they are, then a gin-and-tonic with ice and lemon would be a cocktail – which manifestly it is not. And a straight-up undecorated Dry Martini (two ingredients) would not be a cocktail – which it most decidedly is! In the event, custom and commonsense previal: applied commonsense is better than many a law.

A gallant effort to define "cocktail" was made by Kiamran Halil, barrister-at-law, while he was working in a government department. His unofficial contribution to the debate, in "The New Law Journal" (Feb. 1973), suggested a cocktail is –

". . . a mixture of spirituous liquor (or liquors), in equal or unequal proportions, to which non-alcoholic beverages, fruit juices, bitters, sugar may sometimes be added depending upon individual requirements of recipes (which may also specify the addition of egg whites or yolks, cocktail onions, olives or fruit peel) and shaken in a cocktail shaker or stirred in a mixing glass with ice cubes, intact, cracked or crushed, as the case may be, providing that the strength of the said mixture does not fall below 28 degrees proof spirit." That is 16% alcohol: Mr. Halil was using the superseded Sykes system.

This bit of legal fun is an excellent definition: it would be interesting to see it tested in Court!

* * *

THIS IS AN APPROPRIATE PLACE TO INTRODUCE A SECOND SHORT SELECTION OF GIN DRINKS.

GIN DRINKS 2.

Please see Note preceding selection of recipes in previous chapter.

A.1

2 dry gin
1 Grand Marnier or Cointreau
teaspoon lemon juice
half-teaspoon grenadine syrup

Shake and strain.

ACE

1½ dry gin
½ grenadine syrup
1½ cream
teaspoon egg white

Shake and strain.

ADAM & EVE

1 dry gin
1 Forbidden Fruit liqueur
1 cognac
teaspoon lemon juice

Shake and strain.

I would not normally mix gin and brandy, but this works. I wish the American liqueur, Forbidden Fruit, was more widely distributed in Britain.

ADDISON

1½ dry gin
1½ red vermouth

Shake and strain. Optionally, decorate with cherry.

This is virtually a Martini (Sweet); see previous chapter.

ADIOS AMIGOS

1 dry gin
½ brandy
½ white rum
½ red vermouth
½ lemon juice

Shake and strain.

The title might translate only too literally unless you are sure your friends like this sort of thing.

ALASKA (1)

2 dry gin
1½ lemon juice
teaspoon caster sugar

Shake and strain into tall glass. Float on top teaspoon raspberry syrup or crème de cassis.

ALASKA (2)

1½ dry gin
½ yellow Chartreuse

Shake and strain.

These two very contrasting recipes with identical titles are a prime example of dichotomy in cocktail nomenclature.

ALEXANDER'S SISTER

1 dry gin
1 fresh cream
1 crème de menthe

Shake and strain.

see Alexander: previous chapter.

BEE'S KNEES

2 dry gin
1 lemon juice
1 clear honey

Shake and strain.

BLIMLET

2 dry gin
2 Rose's lime juice cordial
1 lemon juice
½ crème de cassis

Serve on-the-rocks in wine glass.

This is my personal mutation of the Gimlet. It is perfectly satisfactory to use real blackcurrant syrup (not synthetic flavouring) instead of the crème.

BLUE SKY

1½ dry gin
1½ fresh lime (lemon) juice
1½ blue curaçao
½ maraschino

Shake and strain.

There are numerous blue-titled cocktails. They mostly taste fine, but their appeal rests on personal chromatic appreciation: azure is not highly considered in potables. Blue curaçao is the only drink of that colour with any standing. Colour has little to do with flavour: a mix of any desired hue can be produced by employing unflavoured food-colourings.

BULLDOG HIGHBALL

2 dry gin
1½ fresh orange juice

Pour on to ice cubes in tall glass. Top with ginger ale.

DUBONNET

1½ dry gin
1½ Dubonnet
teaspoon lemon juice

Shake and strain.

How good the simple often is.

FALLEN ANGEL

2 dry gin
1 lemon juice
half-teaspoon crème de menthe

Shake and strain.

FLUFFY DUCK

1½ dry gin
1½ advocaat
1 fresh orange juice
1 Cointreau

Mix on-the-rocks in large glass. Top with soda-water.

From Sydney, Australia

FRENCH KISS

2 dry gin
1½ Cointreau
½ lemon juice

Shake and strain.

GAIQUIRI

2 dry gin
1 white rum
1 fresh lime juice
1 grenadine syrup

Shake briskly with crushed ice and strain.

This is manifestly a version (and a powerful one) of the famous Daiquiri. In view of the many modern mutations of this cocktail (raspberry Daiquiris and so on), I have no qualms in printing this excellent version.

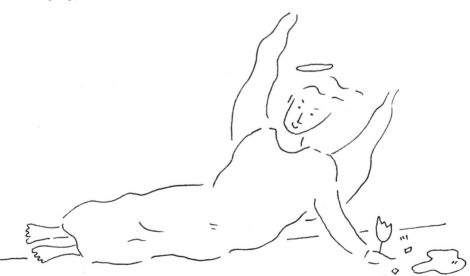

110

GIN-CASSIS

2 dry gin
1½ crème de cassis
teaspoon lemon juice

Shake and strain.

This is a sort of spirituous Kir. You can give it a squirt of soda-water if you want it longer.

GIN PUNCH

2 dry gin
heaped teaspoon caster sugar
¼ pint (150 ml) milk

Shake briskly and stain into tall glass. Dust with nutmeg.

GIN REVIVER

2 dry gin
4 tomato ketchup
teaspoon Worcester sauce
½ lemon juice
dash of Tobasco
sprinkle of celery salt

Shake briskly and strain on to ice cubes in large tumbler. Dash on top a little cayenne pepper. Serve with stick of celery.

This is a type of zippy Bloody Mary, refreshing and restorative, for devout believers in gin's therapeutic virtues.

JOHN'S BOWL

1 standard bottle dry gin
¼ pint (150 ml) each of Cointreau, cognac and lemon juice
3 tablespoons caster sugar

Mix in adequate bowl or jug(s) with lots of ice cubes. Decorate with rounds of cucumber, orange and lemon. Just prior to serving, add large flagon of fizzy lemonade or equivalent of 7-Up.

KAHLUA DAWN

2 dry gin
1 Kahlua liqueur
½ lemon juice

Shake and strain. Serve with cocktail cherry.

LAST TANGO

1½ dry gin
1 orange juice
½ dry vermouth
½ red vermouth
½ Cointreau

Shake and strain.

LICHEE

1½ dry gin
1½ dry vermouth
2 lichee syrup (from canned lichees)
2 dashes Angostura

Shake and strain. Decorate with lichee on stick.

Surplus syrup from canned fruit is very useful for d.i.y. mixed drinks: they all go splendidly with gin.

GIN SIDECAR

2 dry gin
1 lemon juice
1 Cointreau

Shake and strain.

This is a frank mutation of a brandy mix, but it is a good one.

111

GIN SOUTH

1½ dry gin
1 Southern Comfort liqueur
½ lemon juice
½ grapefruit juice

Shake and strain.

GOLDEN FIZZ

1½ dry gin
1 lemon juice
teaspoon caster sugar
yolk (only) of an egg

Shake briskly and strain. Top with soda-water.

GORDON'S CUP

2 dry gin
2 port wine

Pour on-the-rocks in tall glass. Top with 7-Up or fizzy lemonade. Garnish with rounds of lemon and cucumber and sprig of mint in season.

IDEAL

2 dry gin
1 dry vermouth
teaspoon each of lemon juice and maraschino

Shake and strain.

See Perfect (Chapter 8). There are many Ideal cocktails.

LONDONER

2 dry gin
1½ rose-hip syrup
2 lemon juice
½ dry vermouth

Shake and strain.

Rose-hip syrup is a delicious alternative to grenadine — if you don't mind depriving the infants!

NINETEENTH HOLE

1½ dry gin
1 dry vermouth
teaspoon red vermouth
dash of Angostura

Stir and strain. Serve with impaled green olive.

NINETEEN-TWENTY

1 dry gin
1 dry vermouth
1 kirsch
dash of Pernod

Shake and stain.

NUPTIAL BLISS

1½ dry vermouth
½ kirsch
teaspoon each of Cointreau, orange juice, lemon juice

Shake and strain.

ORANGE BLOSSOM
(or GOLDEN GATE)

2 dry gin
2 fresh oragne juice
half-teaspoon caster sugar

Shake and strain.

SALTY DOG

Frost rim of glass by moistening and dipping into table salt until well coated. Without disturbing frosting, pour in one part dry gin to two parts fresh grapefruit juice. Stir carefully, add ice and stir again. Drink through the salt.

I am indebted for this oddity to the celebrated English author, bon vivant, and drinks writer par excellence, Kingsley Amis. He discovered it in Nashville, Tennessee, and claims it is an admirable outdoors drink.

113

SHEEP DIP

2 dry gin
1½ dry sherry
3 strong sweet cider

Stir and strain

A blend of gin and cider tends to pack a hidden power.

SOUTH OF THE BORDER

1½ dry gin
1 lemon juice
1 Kahlua
white of an egg

Shake briskly and strain. Decorate with cherry.

In evolving this, I was surprised to discover how well gin blends with delightful Kahlua, the coffee-rich Mexican liqueur. Perhaps I should have called the cocktail something like Femina: the Kahlua factory is entirely managed by women executives.

XANTHIA

1½ dry gin
1 dry vermouth
1 Cointreau

Mix and serve on-the-rocks.

11

_G_IN IN THE _K_ITCHEN

As an amateur cook of more enterprise than knowledge, I was aware that juniper plays a role in food preparation: for instance, it forms part of the brine for the best smoked salmon. However, I suspected that gin itself, so versatile in other respects, could be more important to the culinary arts than I appreciated or that cookbooks told me.

But I fruitlessly pursued further enlightenment, except for the stray recipe of dubious utility, until I recalled a certain once celebrated restaurant. That was The Duck, at Pet Bottom, a remote location in the environs of Canterbury. This formerly humble bucolic pub was turned, by John and Ulla Laing, into a gastronomic mecca, supreme in Kent and not surpassed (other than in extraneous fripperies) by any restaurant in Britain. John had learned the craft of Mine Host at the smart Guinea Grill in London: Ulla, a beautiful and ebullient Swede, had the inherent skills of a born _chef de cuisine_ – an innovator, not a follower of others.

The celebrities who flocked to The Duck (by no means easy to find) were not there to meet fellow-celebrities or be photographed for gossip columns – a press photographer would have been shown the door – but were persons who wished, unrecognised, to eat superb and original meals in a tranquil setting. When I say that European Royalty – real, not ex-royalty – flew his private plane over to England just to relish one of Ulla's dinners, I am not making up one of my tales. Ulla gained a star in the first British _Guide Michelin_: it was a long time before another woman did. She became herself a celebrity more famous than most of her customers, with appearances on TV and ancillary publicity.

It was a sad day for many a bon vivant when, after twenty years, Ulla hung up her skillet and John relinquished the keys of The Duck's venerable cellar.

I am privileged – you are fortunate – that Ulla was persuaded, for love of her craft, to take time off from the garden, which is the joy of her energetic "retirement", to evolve and test the remarkable recipes that follow. They are all her own inventions. *Bon apppétit.*

NOTE: Measures – Teacup = approx. 7 fl.oz/200 ml. Coffee cup = approx. 5 fl.oz/150 ml. Tablespoon = 15 ml. Teaspoon = 5 ml.

GIN RECIPES (4 PEOPLE THROUGHOUT)

STARTERS

GRAPEFRUIT GINAIGRETTE

2 large pink grapefruit
1 teacup (7 fl ozs/200 ml) strips of smoked Kassler (smoked pork loin)
1 teacup (7 fl ozs/200 ml) diced Appenzell or Gruyere cheese
Fresh herbs such as basil, chives and parsley
Large lettuce heart
Few raspberries if available
Ginaigrette (see below).

Halve the grapefruit and take out segments with a sharp knife. Remove all visible pith and chill the cups. Put segments, cheese, Kassler, herbs in a bowl and turn well with a good dousing of Ginaigrette. Line the cups with overlapping lettuce leaves and pile in the salad. Crown with a raspberry, chill, and serve with wholemeal toast.

GINAIGRETTE

1 coffee cup (15 fl ozs/150 ml) olive oil
⅓ coffee cup (2 fl ozs/50 ml) gin
A little (teaspoon) wine vinegar
Few drops of lemon juice
1 teaspoon mustard powder
½ teaspoon granulated sugar
½ teaspoon salt
½ teaspoon ground white pepper.

Mix dry ingredients first and then gradually whisk in the rest.

PATÉ WITH A GAMEY FLAVOUR

1 teacup (7 fl ozs/200 ml) chicken livers finely minced
1 coffee cup (5 fl ozs/150 ml) fresh pork belly, finely minced
1 egg
1 coffee cup (5 fl ozs/150 ml) double cream
1 coffee cup (5 fl ozs/150 ml) gin
1 tablespoon grated orange peel
1 teaspoon ground allspice
1 teaspoon dried marjoram
2 garlic cloves
Salt & ground black pepper
Butter

Make a paste of crushed garlic and salt on a carving board. (Salt enhances the flavour of garlic.) Mix all ingredients bar the cream and egg and leave to marinate overnight in refrigerator. Thoroughly butter a terrine, beat the egg and cream together, mix them with the marinade and pack them into the terrine. Sprinkle flakes of butter on top and bake for 45 minutes to 1 hour at Gas mark 6/ 200°C/400°F. Cool. Serve in the terrine or turn out on a platter garnished with orange segments and watercress. Never line a terrine with bacon because it detracts from all other flavours

PUSSY PUFFS

1 sheet puff pastry (packs now sold in 'sheets')
1 teacup (5 fl ozs/150 ml) chopped smoked salmon pieces
1 ripe avocado halved, stoned, peeled and cubed
1 tablespoon gin
1 tablespoon fresh lemon juice
Fresh coriander
Egg sauce (see below)

Cut one sheet of pastry into four, brush with egg and cook as instructed. When they have risen, take the 'lid' off each square with a sharp knife and keep warm while allowing the bottom halves to keep on cooking until also golden. Meanwhile steep the smoked salmon in a bowl with the gin and lemon juice.

Egg sauce:
3 egg yolks
2 tablespoons gin
2 tablespoons lemon juice
1 teaspoon white wine vinegar
1 teacup (5 fl ozs/150 ml) melted butter
1 teacup (5 fl ozs/150 ml) double cream
Pinch of caster sugar
Salt.

Boil together gin, lemon juice, vinegar and sugar. Whisk yolks in the top of a double saucepan and add gin-mixture slowly, still whisking vigorously to stop it curdling. On a lower heat, still whisking, gradually add melted butter. Take off heat and whisk in cream. Add avocado and salmon mixture sprinkled with a teaspoonful of coriander and heat through.
  Put lower pastry halves on four warmed plates. Pour in the mixture. Top with remaining lids. Surround with finely-shredded iceberg lettuce and sliced tomato salad Ginaigrette (see first recipe).

QUICK AMBROSIAL STARTER

2 tins of your favourite consommé
Large tablespoon baby prawns
Large tablespoon petit pois
Large tablespoon cooked rice
Parsley & chives
Gin

Put prawns, petit pois and cooked rice in a warmed bowl with gin to cover. Heat well but never *boil* consommé. Have hot serving bowls ready and put a spoonful of gin-saturated mixture in each. Fill up with consommé and sprinkle with parsley and chives. Serve with wholemeal croutons.

SCANDINAVIAN GRAVAD (SWEDISH RAW FISH), HALIBUT OR TURBOT

Thick cut of chosen fish, skinned and boned
Juice of 2 fresh limes
2 tablespoons chopped dill
1 tablespoon caster sugar
Oil
Salt & ground white pepper
Gin

Firm up fish in a freezer for a short time so that you can cut it thinly slantwise with a sharp knife (as for smoked salmon). Arrange the slices overlapping on a platter and sprinkle with salt, a little sugar, and pepper.

Make a marinade of 1 part gin, 1 part fresh lime juice, 1 part oil, the chopped dill and the remaining sugar. Mix well, pour over the fish, cover, and leave overnight. Serve with buttered rye bread and a salad of shredded lettuce and red peppers.

MAIN DISHES – FISH

SHELLFISH STEW

½ lb/250 g Monkfish, skinned, boned and cubed (but keep skin & bone)
1 bag moules ⎫
1 bag cockles ⎬ Young's frozen
1 bag prawns ⎭
Small pack frozen petit pois
2 eggs
¼ lb/100 g sliced button mushrooms, lightly fried
10 fl ozS double cream
Shell-shaped pasta
Finely-grated parmesan
Ground white pepper
Celery salt
Curry powder
Cayenne
Gin
Court-bouillon

COURT-BOUILLON

1 carrot
1 onion
Celery
Lemon juice
Liquid of defrosted shellfish
Dash of gin
Salt & pepper.

Make a courtbouillon with the above ingredients and the skin and bone of the monkfish. Poach the monkfish in this.

In the top of a large double saucepan, pour whisked eggs and add double cream, celery salt, ground white pepper, a pinch each of cayenne and curry powder and 2 tablespoons of gin whilst still whisking. Add some of the court-bouillon and continue to whisk vigorously until it thickens. Add drained monkfish, shellfish and peas and heat through. Sprinkle with finely-chopped green foliage of spring onions and serve with cooked pasta-shells and parmesan.

SMOKED SALMON TARTARE

1 teacup (7 fl ozs/200 ml) finely chopped smoked salmon
2 large finely chopped hard-boiled eggs
1 tablespoon finely chopped sweet gherkins
1 tablespoon finely chopped capers
1 tablespoon finely chopped dill

Mix in a bowl with *Sauce:*
1 coffee cup (5 fl ozs/150 ml) home-made mayonnaise
1 coffee cup thick natural yoghourt
1 teaspoon mustard powder
1 teaspoon caster sugar
Pinch of ground allspice
Pinch of ground aniseed
Salt & pepper
2 tablespoons gin

Fold all together, press into well-oiled moulds and chill well. Serve new potatoes rolled in butter and sprinkled with chopped chives and with fresh green haricot beans.

GAME & MEAT

COQ AU GIN

1 large cock-pheasant, quartered
4 rashers green bacon, diced
½ lb/250 g open field mushrooms, sliced
4 leeks
Flour
Juniper berries
Bayleaf
Handful finely chopped parsley
Coriander
Pepper & salt
Gin

Make a stock from the giblets. Turn pheasant quarters in seasoned flour. Lightly sauté onion bacon and mushrooms and add a coffee cup (5 fl ozs/150 ml) of gin and a teacup (7 fl ozs/200 ml) of the giblet stock.

Put pheasant in a roasting tin with bayleaf, herbs and a few whole juniper berries, pour over the stock and roast, uncovered, at Gas 7/220°C/425°F for 30 minutes. Add chunks of leek and extra stock if necessary, cover, and continue to cook at Gas 5/190°C/375°F for a further 20 minutes. Serve with pommes croquette and celeriac à la crème.

DRUNKEN DUCK

1 plump 3½ lb/1½ kg domestic duck with backbone removed (but keep backbone)
Flour
Zest of ½ grapefruit
1 small onion
Butter
Oil
Celery salt
Black peppercorns
Mixed herbs
Rosemary leaves
Lavender leaves
Gin

Make a julienne of the zest of grapefruit and steep overnight with half a finely chopped onion and gin to cover. Joint the duck and dust well with seasoned flour and with herbs added. Seal lightly in butter and oil in a hot non-stick frying pan and place in an oven-proof dish.

In the same pan pour a good measure of gin (3 fl ozs/75 ml) into the fat-residue and a coffee cup (5 fl ozs/150 ml) of stock made from the backbone and giblets. Let this simmer for a few minutes. Then sieve the steeped grapefruit mixture over the duck, add a few fresh rosemary and lavender leaves, cover, and cook for 30 minutes at Gas 8/230°C/450°F and then lower to Gas 5/190°C/375°F for another 20 minutes. Bring to the table and, at the ultimate serving moment, enhance sauce with a shot (1 fl oz/25 ml) of gin. Serve with pommes noisette and braised chicory.

PARTRIDGE OR PIGEON EN GELÉE

2 birds of your choice
1 can consommée

Julienne of half a thin-skinned lemon
1 tablespoon lemon juice
1 tablespoon butter
Small pack gelatine
2 cloves
Rosemary leaves
1 coffee cup (5 fl ozs/150 ml) gin
Celery salt and pepper
Jar of cranberry sauce

Quarter and bone the birds. Put in deep ovenproof dish. Heat the lemon juice in the consommée with seasonings and julienne and sprinkle the gelatine over. Stir and pour on to game in the dish, adding butter. Cover with foil and cook at Gas 7/220°C/425°F for about an hour, remembering that pigeons take longer than partridge. Remove from oven and pour in gin to mix with the juices. Let cool and then chill, allowing the butter to make a seal. Serve with gin-flavoured cranberry sauce, one soup spoon to a small jar, waffle potatoes and spinach en branches.

KIDNEYS FLAMBÉ (A very quick recipe)

4 large veal kidneys
5 fl ozs double cream
Seasoned flour
Butter
Oil
Gin

Halve kidneys and turn in seasoned flour. Heat oil and butter until smoking in a non-stick pan. Add kidneys, turn after a few seconds, pour in gin (3 fl ozs/25 ml) and set alight. Douse with cream and *then* add a little salt and pepper. Cook for a few more minutes. Serve on hot plates sprinkled with a little parsley and with a good risotto. Delicious with a braised celery in ginaigrette (see above) served apart.

TOURNEDOS ANGOSTURA FLAMBÉ AU GIN

4 thick Tournedos

Fresh green peppercorns
Butter
Celery salt
Ground white pepper
Angostura bitters
Gin

Insert a sharp knife in the side of each tournedos to make a small pocket. Stuff with a coffee spoonful of fresh green peppercorns and press well down. Season with a little pepper and douse well with Angostura bitters. Fry in butter until just rare, sprinkle with celery salt, and then flambé with a large shot (4 fl ozs/125 ml) of gin. Serve on round croutons with the juices poured over, garnished with watercress and a few chicory leaves. Present with pommes paille and barely-cooked mangetout.

SWEET DISHES

GIN & TONIC SORBET

1 large gin & tonic
2 egg whites
1 coffeespoon finely grated zest of lemon
2 tablespoons icing sugar

Whisk egg whites and sugar into a peak. Combine with gin and tonic and zest. Whisk vigorously. Put into a container and freeze. But, *during the freezing process*, it is *essential* to whisk at intervals at least five or six times to combine the egg-white properly with the gin and tonic.

GORDON'S DELIGHT

2 eggs
10 fl oz extra thick double cream
2 tablespoons instant coffee granules
3 tablespoons icing sugar
3 tablespoons Gin

Whisk eggs and whip cream to a peak. Work

Beat egg yolks with sugar until white and foamy. Gradually add the gin. Serve peaches with a little of the syrup in individual dishes and with the egg toddy poured over. Sprinkle with a few toasted crushed hazelnuts.

MA LAING'S GINNY PRUNES

½ lb/225 g large best prunes
2 tablespoons granulated sugar
1 coffee cup ground almonds
1 egg white
Butter
Cold tea
Madeira cake
Gin

Soak prunes in tea overnight just to cover, and keep resulting liquid. Make a thick paste with almonds, whisked egg white and a little sugar. Dry and de-stone prunes, stuff with paste, and seal. Make a syrup with one coffee cup of the tea and the rest of the sugar and, when cook, add 3 fl ozs/75 ml gin. Steep prunes in syrup overnight. Fry four rounds of madeira cake lightly in butter, place the prunes on these, and pour over some of the syrup. A small ladle of gin-laced whipped double cream enhances this concoction.

the coffee, sugar and gin into the eggs. Fold this mixture into the cream, put into rame-kins, and freeze. At the moment of serving, lace with a little gin and sprinkle with a few coffee granules.

INTOXICATED PEACHES

4 large ripe peaches
1 coffee cup (5 fl ozs/150 ml) preserving sugar
1 clove
3 Allspice berries
1 pint (575 ml) water
3 large tablespoons gin
Ginny Egg Toddy

Make a syrup with the water, sugar, clove and allspice berries. Allow to cool and add the gin. Meanwhile plunge the peaches into boiling water and then peel, halve and stone them. Bottle the peaches and syrup and chill them for a few days

Serve with home-made *Ginny Egg Toddy:*
4 egg yolks
3 tablespoons icing sugar
1 coffee cup (5 fl ozs/150 ml) gin

PÈCHES FARCIE

4 large peaches
Small pack of marzipan
2 teaspoons caster sugar
Soft white breadcrumbs
Butter
1 coffee cup (5 fl ozs/150 ml) gin

Treat peaches as for Intoxicated Peaches and put on each one half a knob of marzipan. Cover with a mound of soft breadcrumbs and dot with flakes of butter. Place on a heat-proof serving platter under a very hot grill until the breadcrumbs are golden. Then sprinkle the sugar over them, pour warm gin over and set alight. Don thick white gloves and rush the flaming dish triumphantly to the table! Serve with chocolate langues de chat.

SAVOURY

PANCAKES

12 small pancakes made with your favourite batter
Stuffing:
3 very ripe bananas
½ red pepper
1 large cooking apple
1 small onion
2 tablespoons preserving sugar
Aniseed
1 teaspoon curry powder
1 teaspoon salt
Ground white pepper
Oil
Grated cheese
Gin

Finely chop banana, apple, onion and pepper. Fry in a little oil to cover pan. Add sugar, aniseed and rest of seasoning and cook until firm. Lace with a little (1 fl oz/25 ml) gin, spread a tablespoonful of the mixture on each pancake, roll up, fold in ends and put on a greased heatproof platter. Sprinkle with grated cheese, pour a little gin over, put under grill until cheese melts and serve hot with a crisp salad.

PRESERVES

APRICOT PRESERVE

1 pack large dried Turkish apricots
1 teacup (7 fl ozs/200 ml) preserving sugar
3/4 whole allspice berries
Gin

Soak apricots in water and a little gin overnight. Keep liquid. Warm the sugar over a low heat in a dry, heavy pan. Raise heat and add a coffee cup of the liquid. Stir until sugar is melted. Add apricots and let come to the boil. Lower heat and simmer until 'jammy'. Cool. Bottle in hot jars with two tablespoonfuls of gin and the allspice berries. This is delicious in Omelette Confiture.

LIME PRESERVE

8 limes
1 teacup (7 fl ozs/200 ml) preserving sugar
3 cloves
½ litre/20 fl ozs water
Gin

Halve and thinly slice limes. Steep overnight in gin and water just to cover with a little sugar sprinkled over. Warm preserving sugar in a heavy, dry pan over a low heat. Add a coffee cup (5 fl ozs/150 ml) of gin and water in a ratio of 1 to 4. Simmer until sugar is dissolved. Add steeped limes and continue to simmer slowly, stirring until the limes are tender and the syrup thickens. Bottle in hot jars and seal.

* * *

"Water, taken in moderation, cannot hurt anybody."

Mark Twain

* * *

"I'm quite in favour of temperance propaganda, providing it doesn't unduly restrict the sale of intoxicating liquor."

St. J. Hankin

12

BYEWAYS OF GIN

There are several related topics, additional facts and comments, and emphasis on a couple of points, that I have not had occasion to place in previous chapters.

DUTCH GINS

Geneva, Genever, or Hollands (the official British name) now differ so markedly from London dry gin as effectively to constitute a different product group. Yet they are indeed gin, and we gin-drinkers owe historical homage to the Netherlands.

Broadly, Dutch gins are based on a heavy and powerful alcohol, *moutwijn* ("malt wine"), mainly produced from malted barley. This comes from big distilleries in Schiedam, who use it themselves and also sell it to other distilleries for flavouring with juniper and botanicals to their own gin recipes. *Oude* (old) Genever has a higher proportion of *moutwijn* than the *jonge* (young), descriptions indicating historical, not actual, age. There are also Genevers distilled directly from juniper and highly redolent of its character, too much for most palates and possibly the closest to the spirit distilled by old Sylvius of Leyden. There are a hundred or so brands of Genever, all much more aromatic than dry gin. They are primarily for drinking straight as *schnapps*, often with a beer chaser. They are not mixing spirits and have no place in modern cocktails.

Spirits closely akin to Dutch gins are made in Belgium, *jenever*, and are popular in Germany as *wacholder*, also called Steinhäger after the town particularly renowned for this pungent style.

* * *

123

Juniper is compounded with spirit in many countries. In the Balkans direct distillation from a juniper base is quite popular, such as the Slovakian Borovicka. These pungent spirits hold little appeal outside their lands of origin.

ON THE STAGE

I don't know when gin was first mentioned in a play: it could easily have been in some 18th century drama. So far as cocktails are concerned, someone may be able to say when there was a reference to them in an American play. As to London, the pioneer appearance of a cocktail as a theatrical prop was in 1925, in _Spring Cleaning_ by the fashionable playwright, Frederick Lonsdale. This was quickly followed by Noël Coward's sensation-provoking _The Vortex_, which featured four cocktails. His next, _Fallen Angels_, was awash with booze. Noël epitomised the Cocktail Age, and many of his lyrics hymned the joys of gin and cocktails. In our own times, T. S. Eliot's much-acclaimed psychological play, _The Cocktail Party_, had its enigmastic guest praising, not cocktails, but gin – with water.

In my book on the Dry Martini, I recounted an amusing item of theatrical business related to this subject. In the Broadway production of _Auntie Mame_, with Beatrice Lillie in the title role, she showed her nephew how to make a Martini. Having filled a mixing-glass with a whole bottle of vermouth, she then tossed all this out of the window, and refilled the glass with a bottle of gin.

MAHOGANY

I was ignorant of this until asked to find out by a scion of the peerage: I investigated through curiosity, not snobbery! It is a late 18th century dialect word from Cornwall, describing a mixture of gin and black treacle. I suspect it was medicinal in purpose.

PIMM'S

Of all spin-offs from gin this is the most famous, and rightly so. Insomuch as it first appeared as Pimm's No.1 Cup, The Original Gin Sling, and since a Gin Sling is a cocktail, it could be claimed that Pimm's was the world's first bottled cocktail, ante-dating by a generation the pre-mixed cocktails of Gilbert and Louis Heublein. But I will leave the honours in that field with Hartford, Conn. Pimm's is too special to categorise alongside any other product in its field.

In 1841, James Pimm opened an oyster bar in the City of London. He became celebrated for the gin slings he served there. It was about thirty years later that James Pimm's successors bottled his recipe and sold to other restaurants. Along with London gin, Pimm's found its way into outposts of Empire: the first export order was for Ceylon (Sri Lanka). Overseas sales owed much to the energy of Sir Horatio Davies. He was Lord Mayor of London, 1897–98: significantly, 1898 was the year of the Battle of Omdurman, and it is known that cases of Pimm's were taken up the Nile to refresh Kitchener's officers. I ask myself if young Winston Churchill drank it after returning from that historic cavalry charge.

Devotees of Pimm's have their own little quirks in its preparations. These are not relished by the proprietors who insist it is best made according to the simple instructions on the label. Once a distinctly up-market drink, Pimm's has been skilfully promoted recently and is to be found everywhere: unfortunately, bars continue to tart it up with all sorts of garbage, turning a delicious long drink into a lightly alcoholic fruit salad. Customers have played their part by expecting this decorative over-kill. I admit to giving my Pimm's – best served in a silver tankard – fortification with extra gin and a measure of Cointreau. Strangely, though every aspect of Pimm's has American appeal, it has never done as well in the U.S.A. as it deserves: American hostesses, please note – a Pimm's garden, or pool-side party is the tops!

PLYMOUTH GIN

A gin distillery was established here by the Coates family in 1793. Naturally, gin from the great port became particularly associated with the Royal Navy and thus with Pink Gin. This Devon gin retained a more aromatic flavour after London had revolutionised the trade with triumphant dry gin. Badly damaged in World War II, the company made the mistake of continuing production using inferior spirit: they were not unique in this error. It almost killed the brand. After the war, Plymouth Gin was revived, but it had lost its special hold on a section of gin-drinkers. Under new ownership, the formula was lightened and the brand re-launched: its popularity is largely local. It is now a reputable dry gin, of historical renown.

As to Pink Gin, though it was widely conceded that was properly made only with the (old) Plymouth Gin, some found it too pungent. Writing of Pink Gin, former Royal Navy senior officer Anthony Hogg, in his *Cocktails and Mixed Drinks*, recalls an Admiral of legendary capacity, of whom it was said: "Stick a label of Gordon's on his chest and you could sell him for five shillings and ninepence" [the then duty-free price of a bottle of gin].

* * *

A sidelight on this subject:

I am indebted to Henry McNulty (*Drinking In Vogue*) for the following – which he calls Solid Pink Gin. I feel it deserves a fancier title, the sort of thing you might see on the over-priced menu of a pretentious restaurant: how about *Gelée rose parfumée à l'eau de vie de geniévre?* Henry's recipe:

Make a gelatine according to instructions, replacing water with same quantity of gin to which sufficient Angostura has been added to render it pinkish. Refrigerate. Serve in glass bowls with small spoons, with a slice of lemon on the side.

Henry suggests improving pistachio ice-cream by pouring gin over it, as one might a sauce. Sloe gin gives special character.

SLOE GIN

This is one liqueur that may very satisfactorily be made at home. There are two or three excellent British and American proprietary brands.

Ideally, the sloes should be freshly picked: use soon or they will go mouldy. They are the fruit of the blackthorn and do not occur in profusion every year as there will be few if the frost gets the blossom. (Another function of the blackthorn is to provide its hard wood to make proper shillelaghs.) It is laborious, yet to prick each berry improves results:

Half-fill a large clear bottle with sloes. Add a level 2 inches (5 cms) of caster sugar. Top with good full-strength gin. Close bottle firmly. Shake the bottle(s) as often as you can remember to for three months, or more. Test for sweetness and adjust if necessary. Leave standing for several weeks, the longer the better. Decant carefully, straining if required, into clean bottle(s). The sloe gin will improve further if kept unopened: I swear that one batch I made and kept in litre bottles for two years was better than any other I have tasted.

Sloe gin is delicious on its own, refrigerates well (not too deeply), or may be served on-the-rocks – not too much ice. It is a long-term favourite stirrup-cup at fox-hunting meets. It mixes well with tonic-water, lemonade or 7-Up.

OTHER FRUIT GINS

Orange- and lemon-gins were popular up to 1939 but have virtually disappeared. They can be made much the same way as above. Pare peel carefully from washed fruit so as to avoid pith. Use rather less sugar than for sloe gin and less for orange than for lemon.

Apple gin was once commercialised, and blackberry gin is made in the Netherlands. Damson gin can be pleasing. Almost any fruit can be used, though some (strawberry and raspberry for example) are less suitable than others. Excessive experimentation may simply spoil good gin.

GOOD NEWS

People of a gintellectual bent may be interested to be reminded of the findings of Dr. Gaston Pawan, of London's Middlesex Hospital, a modern pioneer in research into what is commonly referred to as the Hangover. It is not, he maintains, mainly alcohol itself that causes this unpleasant, if temporary, condition: it is congeners that do the damage. He is not speaking of congeners in the sense of those elements that give wines, beers or spirits their taste characteristics, and which in the instance of gin are all wholesome. He is referring to those congeners like amyl alcohols that are formed during fermentation or primary distilling. Some of these disappear during maturing in wood or are totally eradicated by rectification of spirit, such as is the base of gin. In parts per million of congeners (both toxic and harmless), Dr. Pawan puts red wine at the top with 400, then beers with an average of 380, brandy at 352, white wine at 350 – and gin at a mere 3.

TOURISTS BEWARE

When I got to Madrid in the spring of 1946 (after a motor journey of considerable interest), I was entranced by the city's luxury: such a contrast to my austerity-damp London and the war deprivations still ravaging France. I was also delighted that my pound notes, judiciously exchanged, gained me my Ritz Hotel bedroom for the modest equivalent of eleven shillings – 55p – a night. On my first evening, I wandered into a posh bar and sank three substantial Dry Martinis, apparently made from a bottle containing Gordon's export gin. But I was wrong, and spent the next two days confined to that bedroom. My taste-buds temporarily impaired by wartime drought, I had not noticed the spurious gin.

It behoves travellers to be wary in continental bars to this day. In Spain, you are unlikely to suffer as I did in really top class establishments, but beware ordering gin in any sort of "tourist trap" club or similar places. To repeat advice: on your holiday you are recommended to buy a well-known brand in a store (avoiding the suspiciously cheap) and drink on your hotel balcony or villa terrace.

Gin is such a superb base for hot weather holiday mixes that it would be a pity to spoil pleasure for the want of elementary caution.

Speaking of Spain, though my advice goes for many countries, a Spanish peculiarity is

Minorcan Gin

This curious survivor from the days when Minorca was a base for Nelson's fleet is strong, aromatic and an amusing something for visitors to the island to try.

SUB-NORMAL

In chapter 10, the introduction of low-strength spirits in the U.S.A. is commented on. In Britain, there have for some time been gins – without big names – below normal strength (40% alcohol). These "sub-norms" as the trade knows them are sometimes called "cocktail gin". That is a misnomer. For good cocktails you must have full – or over-strength gin: the making of a cocktail is going substantially to weaken the spirit. *Caveat immisceror* (author's Dog Latin for "Let the mixer take care").

"Sub-norm" also applies to bottles of less than standard capacity – 70 cls in place of the customary 75 cls (¾-litre or an American "fifth"). Any apparent saving in buying gin sub-normal in strength and/or quantity is illusory: you pay a little less money and get correspondingly less for it. When in doubt, read the label. To have no doubts, stick to the tried and trusted brands.

VARIOUS GINS OR "GINS"

The word gin has become attached to certain spirits that bear little or no resemblance to the real thing: most of these have no connection with juniper. The most notorious are the "banana gins" of Africa, which are not necessarily made from bananas but from anything that will ferment. *Waragi* and *moshi* are the best-known: popular in Uganda, Tanzania and Kenya. Good examples will not actually poison anyone. Of course, in stable countries like Kenya, sound London dry gin is readily available. You should have no difficulties in the hotels of the international chains that have spread across Africa as in other continents.

AFRICA

Africa has peculiar associations with gin, at an almost magical level. "Trade gin" – probably mostly raw spirit – was an item in early commerce with West African potentates and played its role in the purchase of slaves for transport to the Americas. As a result, gin achieved a place in the rituals of some African nations and libations of gin were poured at the feet of distinguished persons as a sign of respect, to ward off evil influences and bring good fortune. I have in my files a newspaper photograph picturing possibly the last instance of this rite performed on British soil. It shows a Ghanaian sprinkling a bottle of excellent gin on to the tarmac at London Airport just prior to the arrival, in the summer of 1965, of the plane carrying President Nkrumah of Ghana on an official visit to London. In this instance, the traditional ceremony proved ineffectual: the president was shortly afterwards deposed.

THE WORLD

It is no purpose of this book to survey gin's position in the wide world: that would be repetitious and uninteresting. In Canada, Australia, New Zealand, and South Africa, as one would expect, English gin brands prevail. But then they do in less traditionally gin-drinking lands: in France, for instance, most bistros now display gin. In South America, in Brazil and Chile for example, English gin brands are produced, for in all great cities the people who use smart bars are cosmopolitan in their tastes. In the countries of the British Commonwealth, the wealthier folk continue with drinking patterns inherited from the imperial past, and those often include gins at sundown. There is almost nowhere that dry gin, at its best imported from London or made by English firms, cannot be obtained. I have seen a large consignment of gin being loaded on to a Russian ship in the Thames, destined for hard currency shops in the Soviet Union for the delectation of the privileged. Of Britain and the U.S.A. I have written fully.

From its small beginnings, after a long journey, gin spans the globe. I trust we have shown why it deserves its splendid position in the pantheon of great spirits.

London & Camberley,
1934–1989

129

A CKNOWLEDGEMENTS

Over the years I have enjoyed books by the following authors, with some of whom I have exchanged information, particularly in relation to gin. Dates refer to editions on my shelves: I cannot be sure all these books are in print.

Kingsley Amis: ON DRINK (Cape, London, 1972); EVERY DAY DRINKING (Hutchinson, London, 1983)
Lowell Edmunds: THE SILVER BULLET (Greenwood Press, Westport, Conn, 1981)
David A. Embury: THE FINE ART OF MIXING DRINKS (Faber, London, 1953)
Emanuel & Madeline Greenberg: THE POCKET GUIDE TO SPIRITS & LIQUEURS (Perigree Books, New York, 1983)
Harold J. Grossman: GROSSMAN'S GUIDE (Scribner's, New York, 1964)
Marilyn Harper (Editor): U.K.B.G. INTERNATIONAL GUIDE TO DRINKS (Hutchinson, London, 1981)
Anthony Hogg: COCKTAILS & MIXED DRINKS (Hamlyn, London, 1979)
Stan Jones: COMPLETE BARGUIDE (Barguide Enterprises, Los Angeles, 1977)
Tony Lord: THE WORLD GUIDE TO SPIRITS (Macdonald & Jane's, London, 1979)
Henry McNulty: DRINKING IN VOGUE (André Deutsch, London, 1978)

Cyril Ray: THE COMPLETE BOOK OF SPIRITS & LIQUEURS (Cassell, London, 1977)
Andrew Sinclair: PROHIBITION (Four Square, London, 1965)
Brian Spiller: VICTORIAN PUBLIC HOUSES (David & Charles, Newton Abbot, 1972)
John Watney: MOTHER'S RUIN (Peter Owen, London, 1976)
Pamela Vandyke Price: SPIRITS & LIQUEURS (Penguin, London, 1979)

Limited or rare editions:
Eddie Clarke: SHAKING IN THE SIXTIES (private publication, 1963)
Harry Craddock: THE SAVOY COCKTAIL BOOK (1st ed., Constable, London, 1930)
Cedric Dickens: DRINKING WITH DICKENS (C. Dickens, Holton, Wincanton, Somerset, 1980)
Harry Johnson: BARTENDERS' MANUAL (private publication, New York, 1882)
William Juniper: THE TRUE DRUNKARD'S DELIGHT (Unicorn Press, London, 1933)
Lord Kinross: THE KINDRED SPIRIT (Newman Neame, London, 1959)
Oscar A. Mendelsohn: DRINKING WITH PEPYS (Macmillan, London, 1963)
André Simon: DICTIONARY OF WINE, SPIRITS & LIQUEURS (Jenkins, London, 1961)

GINDEX